HAUNTED
NOTTINGHAM
Myths, Magic and Folklore

HAUNTED NOTTINGHAM

Myths, Magic and Folklore

Wayne Anthony

First published in Great Britain in 2008 by
The Breedon Books Publishing Company Limited
Breedon House, 3 The Parker Centre,
Derby, DE21 4SZ.

This paperback edition published in Great Britain in 2014 by DB Publishing,
an imprint of JMD Media Ltd

ISBN 978-1-78091-423-7

Printed and bound in the UK by Copytech (UK) Ltd Peterborough

Contents

Acknowledgements   6

Introduction   7

Telltale Signs of the Dead   9

City of the Dead   10

Hours of the Living   20

Supernature   26

Forbidden Worlds   50

Wraith of Shades   62

Shiver and Shake   69

Echoes in Time   78

The Whispering Dead   125

Residential Ghosts   146

Lexicon Mystique   172

Bibliography   192

Acknowledgements

The author would like to thank the people, who have so willingly opened their hearts, homes and personal histories, and who have allowed him to trample on their lands and take intrusive photographs while the research for this book was underway. A special thank you is due to the people of Nottingham and Nottinghamshire, who have so willingly contributed little-known facts about the culture and heritage of their beloved shire.

The author is particularly grateful to his friends and family for their support, understanding and encouragement while the book was being written.

Introduction

Nottingham, surrounded by its distinct and beautiful shire, lies in the central-eastern part of England and covers an area of approximately 844 square miles. For centuries there were two areas of England that were divided by the River Trent, and this river was at one time a main artery for industrial supply and demand from Nottinghamshire to other parts of the country. Archaeological evidence indicates that some of the first settlers in the county date from 43,000BC. Nottingham is first mentioned in an Anglo-Saxon chronicle dated 867, which mentions the area as 'Snottaingham'. The Saxon word ham means 'village', the word inga means 'belonging to' and Snotta refers to a name; therefore, the village was owned and governed by a man named Snotta. The actual shire of Nottingham was created somewhere between the late ninth and early 11th century and received its county status in 1448 from King Henry VI.

Nottinghamshire has managed to retain a magnificent array of historical items and architecture. Although documented legends and folklore are scarce compared to other areas of the country, there are enough rare and interesting facts about Nottingham and its shire to make it stand out. From its magnificent houses, mansions, parks and woodlands to its cosy villages, fabulous churches and atmospheric castles, all have unique and often curious stories to tell. The history and folklore of these places have undoubtedly helped the area stand out from other regions of England.

During its industrial boom, Nottingham became known for its coal, ceramics, wool dyeing and brewing, and by the mid-18th century it had a thriving textile industry, which was boosted by the growth of cotton and lace manufacturing. With this new demand came a new age for the area as people moved into the shire to take up new jobs and for greater opportunities. With these people came their folklore, magic, myths, ghost stories and superstitious beliefs. Theses ancient beliefs were fused into the existing ones and added to the already colourful legends. This is undoubtedly why there are unmistakeable similarities with some of the stories that we find in other shires of England. Even Robin Hood, Nottingham's most famous legend, is encountered in other areas, often under different names – Father of the Wood, Jack O' the Green, Robin of the Hood.

I am often asked what a ghost is, and it is a question that I find difficult to answer clearly as there are so many contradicting opinions. Maybe it is a terrible event repeating time and time again, or an instant of pain caught within its own eternity. These creatures of shades could be mere recordings of twisted and tragic events long since past. Do the unhappy dead or wraiths exist within the shadows lamenting their untimely departure? Are they waiting for a time to arrive when they can reveal themselves to the living, for reasons known only to themselves? To gain absolution perhaps? To be forgiven for their terrible crimes? To reveal their tragedy to the world, thus enabling them to be released from their trapped state? Who really knows?

So, what is a ghost? Let us immerse ourselves in the following stories of myths, magic and folklore and attempt to find out...

Wayne Anthony
Spring 2008

Telltale Signs of the Dead

Is There a Ghost in Your House?

The 12 Key Signs that Could Indicate a Ghost in your House.

1. You hear unexplained and strange noises.

2. Lights go on and off of their own accord.

3. Electrical equipment continually breaks down.

4. You cannot sleep or wake up in the early hours of the morning with feelings of 'not being alone'.

5. Items are inexplicably moved around.

6. You see something – shadows, shapes – often out of the corner of your eye.

7. Unusual or horrible smells pervade certain areas of the building at certain times.

8. You regularly feel exhausted and unable to concentrate.

9. You are experiencing icy blasts of air or unusual cold areas within the building, or there are radical temperature changes.

10. There are certain times of the day which don't 'feel right' in your home.

11. You feel very uncomfortable in one particular room in the house.

12. Random scratching noises can be heard coming from different rooms or from beneath the floorboards.

City of the Dead

QMC – Queen's Medical Centre, Nottingham

The Queen's Medical Centre, Nottingham University Hospital, is affectionately known as Queen's to the people of the city. The hospital opened its doors to the people in August 1978. This was the first purpose-built teaching hospital in the United Kingdom and was hailed as a massive step forward in healthcare and medicine.

Queen's replaced five hospitals – the Women's Hospital, the General, Harlow Wood Orthopaedic Hospital, the Eye Hospital and the Children's Hospital. These five hospitals had a history of care and medicine in Nottingham which spanned 200 years. Today the QMC offers specialist care to millions of people.

Just after the hospital opened, rumours began to circulate that a strange caped and hooded figure was wandering the corridors at night. Several nurses claimed to have encountered the figure; one nurse, Beverly, confronted the figure near a stairwell on an upper floor, only to find that when it turned around the figure had no face, 'just an empty space where a face should be'. Not content to accept what she had seen, Beverly, thinking that it might be a junior doctor playing tricks, grabbed the figure by its cape, but it dissolved right in front of her eyes.

Soon other medical staff began to complain that they were being mysteriously pinched or slapped when nobody was around. Other staff on night shifts sometimes had a short nap on their official break, and a designated room was set aside for this purpose. Tired doctors working long shifts would also use this room when the wards were quiet. Shortly after settling down for their naps, staff experienced the sensation of being violently shaken, and a female voice with an authoritative tone would shout 'Wake up and get back to work.' Some of the medical staff were so shocked that they immediately did as they were told. Others, thinking it was a dream, attempted to go back to sleep,

The Angel of Death taking the soul.

but the same thing happened again! The room soon got a reputation and became known as the 'Haunted Room.' In the end, staff refused to go in there and would go to another staffroom to have their break.

In another part of the hospital other spooky goings-on were taking place. This time it was a screaming woman. Staff walking past a certain unused room would hear the blood-chilling scream of a woman begging for help. On opening the door and rushing in they would find the room completely empty. One nurse who experienced this phenomenon stated that on opening the door the room was filled with a grey mist.

The Ye Olde Trip to Jerusalem Public House

The Ye Olde Trip to Jerusalem public house is thought to be one of the oldest pubs in England. Local legend maintains that it was built in 1189 and was once visited by Richard the Lionheart. Crusaders also used it as a watering hole on their way to the Holy Land. Much of the building is carved into the rock on which Nottingham Castle stands.

The pub has a unique and happy atmosphere, which is surprising considering the numerous ghosts – some good and some bad – that are supposed to haunt it. Over the years nearly all the landlords have confirmed that the building has ghosts.

In one of the rooms at the inn there is a model of a galleon covered in decades' worth of dust and cobwebs. The galleon is believed to be cursed, and no one is prepared to clean

it for fear of a terrible reprisal, namely a horrible death. Previous managers have claimed that the last three people to have cleaned the ship all met with untimely deaths within the year. The same room is also said to be by far the most haunted. Pitiful crying has been heard emanating from the room when there was no one present, and staff working in the building have frequently reported hearing the sound of breaking glass and on investigating found no evidence of any damage.

There are several other model ships within the building, which, it is said, have been left by sailors who made them to pass away their time at sea. Nottingham once had a busy port, because the River Trent is navigable all the way to the Humber and the North Sea.

The Cursed Galleon. Death and disaster is said to befall all those who clean this enigmatic ship.

Previous landlords would tell tales of their dogs being terrified to enter certain rooms. Cold blasts of air have been reported, coming from the area near the stairs, and in this area the sounds of phantom footsteps have been heard. Some are heavy, as if they were a man's, and some light, as if they belonged to a woman or child. In the cellars a woman in a green crinoline dress has been seen, accompanied by the heavy smell of burning tallow, while in other parts of the building a man dressed in 18th-century attire wanders 'as if looking for something he has lost'.

Also located within the cellars is a small cell, believed by some to be an original condemned cell of Nottingham Castle, which is located almost directly above. A 'feeling of doom' has been felt within this small room, and many people refuse to stay in there for more then a few minutes.

Over the years many so-called mediums have visited the building, adding further stories of ghosts and ghouls to the now legendary haunted pub. Can they be believed? Probably not, but this does not detract from the charm and character of Nottingham's most haunted public house.

Galleries of Justice, Nottingham

The Galleries of Justice, located in the heart of the city's Lace Market, were in use as a prison and court from the late 18th century to the late 20th century. Records reveal that there has been a court on the site since 1375; further research reveals that a prison may also have existed here as early as 1449.

Blind Justice.

At one time this was one of the few places in Britain where you could be tried, convicted and then sentenced. Some records reveal that several criminals were executed at the entrance to the building. The present-day building still retains its original condemned cells and dungeons, as well as two courtrooms and a myriad of caves carved out of the rock.

Over the years there have been many attempts by paranormal investigators to solve the riddle of the numerous ghosts that haunt the building, and it is a regular attraction for would-be paranormal and researchers because of its frequent manifestations and psychic phenomena. The prime areas of activity within the building, to name a few, are as follows:

The Court Room – This is one of the most haunted rooms in the building, perhaps due to the human emotions experienced here over the centuries. Strange groans and cries have been heard emanating from this room, and dark figures have been seen on the balconies. A disembodied hand also appears, only to vanish again. The Court Room is also a hotspot for spirit photography, as orbs and other strange images have been caught on film here.

The Caves/Chapel – Indistinguishable whispers have been heard, things are thrown around and unexplained stones have materialised and been thrown at people in this room, as well as other inexplicable physical phenomena. An evil spirit is said to reside here.

Courtyard/Exercise Yard –This is another hotspot for spirit photography; orbs as well as wispy, grey human shapes have been captured on film. Some convicts who actually died in the prison or were executed are buried here, and several people have claimed to experience the feeling that their ankles and lower limbs have been grabbed by unseen hands.

Cell Corridor – The sound of something being dragged and disturbing thudding noises are frequently heard in this area. Phantom footsteps have been heard and the smell of cheese has been evident here. A jailer who rattles his keys is one of the more frequent apparitions you may encounter.

Entrance Hall – It is said that up to six ghosts haunt this area, including a former guard, a lady in grey and an emaciated man. Cold spots are frequently reported, and one lady claims to have been slapped violently on her bottom!

The Pits – The inexplicable feeling of nausea and an indefinable phantom fragrance are said to accompany the ghost of a woman who wanders this region of the building. Many people have been forced to leave the area for fear of actually being sick. One might also experience a cold blowing wind in the ear, as well as a horrible sensation of being strangled.

In recent times there has been an increase in the number of reports of ghosts being seen, sensed or smelt on the premises. One lady told me that she believed she had encountered the ghost of Oscar Wilde during an exhibition in which the cell door from Reading Gaol, where he had been kept prisoner, was on public display at the Galleries of Justice. She stated 'I looked at the door and the next thing I knew I could see a man stood in front of it…From his appearance and looks I knew that I was looking at the ghost of Oscar…He just looked very sad and lonely…The figure just slowly vanished and I was left with a horrible feeling of depression…' It is an interesting story, but can ethereal ghosts follow or be attached to physical objects? It would seem so, as there have been numerous reports throughout history of ghosts following a physical item or being attached to something physical which had great emotional value or tragic consequences for them.

Ye Olde Salutation Inn

With a history nearly spanning 800 years, the Ye Olde Salutation Inn on Maid Marian Way is one of Nottingham's most haunted pubs. Over the centuries different names have been painted on one of the walls outside. The date AD 1240 is displayed on the apex wall; however, the first building on the site belonged to a tanner, whose workshops were on the ground floor. Other significant dates are as follows:

1440 – Records reveal that a private dwelling existed on the site, which belonged to a John Alastre.

1649–59 – Puritans formed the Commonwealth Government. The authorities were unhappy with the pub sign, which had an archangel saluting the Virgin Mary, so the landlord was ordered to remove the sign. The inn was renamed the Soldier and Citizen.

1660 – At the time of the Restoration of the monarchy, the owner reinstated the name Salutation but let the pub sign of the Soldier and Citizen remain. Eventually, when the sign rotted and fell down, it was replaced by a painting of a handshake.

1937 – Following an investigation by the Thoroton Excavation, it was discovered that the ninth-century caves beneath the pub may well have been inhabited by Saxons.

1992 – Nottingham University's Department of Archaeology's tree-dating labs put a date on the oldest timber in the pub of around 1360.

The innocent spirit (often referred to as Radiants), of a child called Rosie is said to haunt the cellars of the inn. The ghost is said to hide things and, from time to time, can be heard giggling.

The inn's most notorious ghost is that of a little girl, who is seen in the area of the caves. Her name is said to be Rosie, a four-year-old urchin who was run down by a carriage in the 17th century. Although other so-called mediums who have visited the pub have given her names including Lizzy, Mary and Helen, they all tend to agree that she was either murdered or met with a tragic end. The ghost is frequently up to mischief, performing pranks like hiding keys and throwing things around. Another ghost in the pub includes an old man, and the frequent sound of phantom footsteps is also heard.

Nottingham Execution List
The Vengeful Dead

Death claiming the souls of sinners.

Is there any wonder that Nottinghamshire should be one of the most haunted counties in the United Kingdom when we begin to consider some of the terrible executions that took place there? Looking back we cannot be certain that all of the alleged crimes committed were indeed perpetrated by the accused, and even if those accused did commit the crimes they were brought to trial for, we cannot know whether they were actually in a state of mental well-being. I suspect that in many cases these people were mentally ill.

The last public execution to take place in Nottingham was outside the Shire Hall in 1861; Richard Darker was accused and sentenced for killing his mother at Fiskerton. Executions after that time took place in private.

Today the marks of where the gallows once stood still remain. Can we begin to imagine the emotional upset and obvious horror of the people, as terrible crimes like rape, abuse and murder were reported in the local press? Worse than this, what terrible things were being whispered in the farm cottages and workplaces? Is there any wonder that a great frenzy would take place when the perpetrator of a crime was caught or sentenced to death? Many of the executed are still said to haunt the scenes of their crimes, and some of the executions that took place are as follows:

The Devil devouring the souls of the damned and consuming their earthly evil.

1767 – Thomas Reynolds for a robbery in Chesterfield Street, 30 August.

1769 – William Hebb for murder, 30 March.

1773 – Joseph Shaw for burglary, 30 March.

1775 – William Voce for committing a rape at Sneinton, 20 March.

1781 – George Brown, alias Bounds, and Adam Bagshaw for burglary, 28 March.

1784 – Ann Castledine and Robert Rushton for murder, 17 March.

1785 – John Pendrill, John Townsend, John Anderson and William Cook for highway robbery, 23 March.

1786 – William Hands and John Lister for mare stealing, 29 March.

1790 – Samuel Martin and Anthony Farnsworth for burglary, 24 March.

1793 – William Healey for horse stealing, 27 March.

1795 – David Proctor for rape, 25 March.

1797 – John Milner for cow stealing, 16 August.

1800 – John Atkinson for forgery, 16 April.

1801 – Michael Denman, William Sykes and Thomas Bakewell for forgery, 5 August.

1802 – Mary Voce for murder, 15 March.

1803 – John Thompson for robbery, 23 March.

1803 – William Hill was hanged on 10 August for committing a rape (attended with great brutality) on the person of Mrs Sarah Justice, the wife of a respectable farmer, at Bole, near Gainsborough, 28 May.

1805 – Robert Powell, alias Harvey, for robbery, 10 April.

1806 – William Rhodes, alias Davies, for forgery, 26 March.

1812 – Benjamin Renshaw for firing a haystack, 29 July.

1813 – William Simpson for murder, 23 March.

1815 – John Hemstock for murder, 23 March.

1816 – John Simpson, alias Daniel Simpson, for highway robbery, 3 April.

1817 – Daniel Diggle for attempted murder, 2 April.

1818 – George Needham and William Manderville for burglary, 3 April.

1820 – Thomas Wilcox for highway robbery, 29 March.

1822 – Henry Sanderson, Robert Bamford and Adam Adie for murder, 22 March.

1823 – Thomas Roe and Benjamin Miller for robbery, 2 April.

1825 – Thomas Dewey for murder, 27 July

1825 – Samuel Wood for murder, 16 March.

1826 – George Milnes and Joshua Smith for burglary, 26 July.

1827 – William Wells for robbery, 2 April.

1831 – William Reynolds and William Marshall for rape, 24 August.

1833 – William Clayton for murder, 2 April.

1834 – William Hinckley for murder, 23 July.

1836 – Richard Smith for rape, 30 March.

1839 – John Driver for murder, 31 July.

1842 – William Saville for murder, 7 August.

1860 – John Fenton for murder, 1 August.

Nottingham Castle

There is much uncertainty about whether a castle actually existed on the site before the Norman Conquest. William the Conqueror ordered that a castle be built in 1067. It was almost certainly a wooden structure, but in the reign of Henry I, 1100–35, a more architecturally complicated stone structure was erected. For centuries the castle was visited by royalty and nobility; being close to the Royal Hunting Park and within short distance from the River Trent made it a strategic stop-off point.

Today the castle is known for its association with the legendary Robin Hood. During the reign of Richard the Lionheart, and while he was away at the Crusades, the castle, according to legend, was unused and fell into disrepair, only to be occupied by the Sheriff of Nottingham. The legend states that the last battle between Robin Hood and the Sheriff of Nottingham took place at the castle.

On 19 October 1330, shortly before his 18th birthday, Edward III, accompanied by several other trusted noblemen and soldiers, entered Nottingham Castle by a secret cave, now known as Mortimer's Hole. Proceeding to his mother's (Isabella of France) bedroom, where she was with her lover Roger Mortimer, 1st Earl of March, Edward arrested both of them. Isabella and Mortimer had been acting as regents since the murder of Edward's father at Berkeley Castle, but Edward had decided to take back control of what he considered to be his right to be king.

Mortimer was kept in a cell overnight in the castle and then later sent to the Tower of London, where he was executed a month later. Isabella was sent to Castle Rising in Norfolk, where she remained for the rest of her days. Some say that after Mortimer's death she was never the same again, although she is known to have been buried in her wedding dress and interred with Edward's heart!

There are numerous ghosts that haunt the castle, but the most prolific phantoms are those of Isabella and Mortimer. Previous workers at the castle report hearing a woman screaming in French, and the sounds of a scuffle and swords clashing have also been reported. The cell cut into the rock at the base of the castle, known as Mortimer's Hole, is haunted by a dark figure who is seen kneeling, as if in prayer, on certain nights of the year.

The ghosts of Isabella and Mortimer still walk the halls and rooms of the castle.

A castle has stood on this site since 1067. The castle has always been a strategic stop-off point for royalty and nobility moving from one area of the country to another.

Nottingham Castle has passed through numerous phases in history — during the Industrial Revolution the castle stood proud on its majestic mount, and its ghosts have continued to be part of its charisma and charm.

Hours of the Living

Ghostly Highwaymen

The Great North Road enters the county of Nottinghamshire just south of Balderton, then crosses the Fosse Way, a Roman military road, at Newark, then runs through Tuxford and on to Bawtry. It was once the main trunk road to the north during the coaching days, probably due to the fact that it ran through or near to 18 other villages or hamlets, compared to some of the other roads which only passed a handful. Today it has been bypassed by the A1.

The road existed for centuries and was one of the busiest roads in England, with many travellers using it. But with many travellers came many highwaymen, who would stake out certain patches of the road in the knowledge that travellers would be carrying money and valuables. Passengers feared for their lives and often knew better then to fight back when they heard the all too familiar bone-chilling cry 'Your money or your life!' It is no wonder then that this stretch of road has numerous ghosts, and the fact of the matter is that there were several men executed for highway robbery directly connected to the Nottinghamshire area. In recent times one gentleman claims to have seen a headless horseman sat upon a coach and four horses with skeletal bodies and flaming red eyes. 'Onward, onward,' he cries, with his whip mercilessly flogging the phantom horses. They then vanish out of sight, as if the hounds of hell were chasing them.

Another perhaps more famous ghost of the road is 'Owd Lad,' an ancient name said to mean 'horned one'. It is thought to be His Satanic Majesty out and about, especially on moonlit nights, collecting the souls of the damned. He speeds along the road silently in a black coach with four coal-black horses. Woe betide the man or woman who dares call out or attempt to stop Owd Lad, as they will never be seen again.

Yet another well-known ghost of the road is John Nevison (1639–1684), or Swift Nick as he was known; a name which was supposedly bestowed upon him by King Charles II. He is thought to be wearing a tri-cornered hat and dark cloak. A cold dark wind precedes his arrival, and a terrible sense of panic and dread follows in his wake. Those who have encountered the ghost talk about their experience with fear, and one gentleman claims his hair turned completely grey overnight!

Local legend states that it wasn't Dick Turpin who made the famous London to York ride on Black Bess to establish an alibi, a journey that took them 15 hours in total, but that it was Swift Nick. He managed a gang of thieves and highwaymen. They would often meet up at the Talbot Inn in Newark to discuss their felicitous thefts and plan further robberies and heists along the Great North Road, but unfortunately for Nick his luck was about to run out. In 1676 one Elizabeth Burton was arrested for stealing and very soon blabbed to the authorities, no doubt in a bid to save her own neck, giving up the identity of Nevison. The courts found John Nevison guilty and transported him to Tangiers. A few years later he sneaked back into England and soon began his old ways again, but four years later he was finally caught and sentenced to be hanged, at Tyburn near London.

On 15 March 1685 John Nevison climbed the scaffold to the hangman's noose and addressed a crowd of thousands of people who had gathered to watch his execution. He asked others not to follow his path as they, too, would end up where he was standing. The hangman then launched Swift Nick into eternity, and his body was later cut down and transported to York, where it was interred in an unmarked grave.

In 1701 a Lincolnshire-born criminal, Timothy Buckley, aged 29, formerly known to have been a shoemakers' apprentice but who had become an evil and most vile criminal, robbed his way round London before moving north to continue his nefarious ways in Nottinghamshire. He terrorised the highways until one fateful day on the Derby Road, just outside Nottingham, he was apprehended following a ferocious battle. First, Buckley's horse was shot dead by a passenger of a stagecoach with a blunderbuss. Buckley, furious at his beloved horse having been slain, immediately fired back using all eight of his horse pistols. He managed to kill a male passenger and a footman, but eventually he was overcome with weakness from blood loss having been wounded.

After a short trial at Nottingham Shire Hall, Buckley was found guilty and was later hanged. Now, his ghost apparently haunts the roads and leafy lanes of the shire.

Murder Most Foul at Scrooby

The charming rural village of Scrooby, in the extreme north of the county, is a small settlement on the south bank of the River Ryton, surrounded by a number of larger residences near the Great Northern Railway, between Retford and Bawtry. The name Scrooby originates from Scandinavia; the first part refers to a personal name, possibly a man named Skorri, and the second part to his farm or hamlet. The variations in spelling were: Scrobi, Scroby, Scrobia and Scrowby.

Scrooby was once the seat of the Archbishops of York; curiously enough, in its old archiepiscopal mansion, the leaders of the pilgrim fathers completed their project for colonising New England. The village also occupied an important position in the coaching days, for it was on the Great North Road, which ran from London through the village of Scrooby to York and eventually terminated at Edinburgh. For a considerable length of time before the toll gate was established at Scrooby, the Great North Road was a badly kept unenclosed tract through open country. In 1555 Parliament passed an Act requiring every parish to elect two surveyors to keep the highways in repair by forced labour, but it had little effect.

Even in 1700 it is said that it took up to a week to travel from London to York on the Great North Road. An Act was passed in 1766 which stated that the local 'narrow and ruinous' roads, which could not be sufficiently repaired, should be widened and kept in repair by the ordinary course of law. This was not possible, and the local parish councils complained that they could not afford to maintain the road in the fashion that the government required. The objections were partly listened to, and Parliament finally agreed to allow companies as well as individuals to take over the maintenance of the roads and charge a small toll to users. Pikes were often used as a barrier to bar access along the road, but a small fee allowed the traveller through to continue their journey. The use of these pikes gave rise to the term turnpike, a phrase that is still used today.

It was at Scrooby that a terrible murder took place in 1779. There once existed a toll gate just outside the village, run by Mary Yeadon and her son William. One dark night at Scrooby Toll Gate, just after Mary and William had retired to bed, local man John Spencer decided to relieve the Yeadons of their toll gate earnings. Entering into the house, he attempted to make off with the strongbox, but unfortunately for all involved he made too much noise, no doubt due to the rattling of the coins within the box, which roused Mary and William from their sleep. A local document records the following:

1779 – John Spencer, a native of North Leverton, was executed at Nottingham, on the 26 July, for the murder of William Yeadon, and his mother, Mary Yeadon, the keepers of Scrooby toll-bar, near which place his body was hung in chains; the gibbet post still remaining. A few weeks after being hung in chains, a party of soldiers passed that way, when a serjeant fired a musket, loaded with ball, at the body, and hit it. As soon as the circumstance was known, the soldiers were pursued, and the serjeant taken. He was afterwards tried by a court martial, and turned into the ranks.

Close inspection of the local parish records for 1779 further reveals that in the right hand of the corpse was placed the hedge stake with which John Spencer had bludgeoned to death his victims!

Shortly after this event, reports began to emerge of a ghostly cloaked figure seen walking close to the site of the old toll gate. There have been reports of motorists who have stopped to give the phantom person a lift, believing he or she to be a hitchhiker, but the figure vanishes into thin air! Phantom screams and odd bumping sounds are still said to be heard on the road close to the site of the execution of John Spencer. One ghostly report tells of visions of a cottage, emerging out of a strange mist, in which a candle can be seen burning in the window. On approaching the cottage, terrible screams and thudding noises can be heard, and the cottage then vanishes. One gentleman, having had a nocturnal experience at the site of the toll gate, returned the next day to find no signs of a cottage anywhere.

To Be or Not to Be – Superstitions

Very few people in England manage to get through a week without making some kind of reference to a superstition, be these ancient superstitions, such as walking under a ladder, the spilling of salt, crossing on a stairway or a black cat crossing your path, or some more modern day superstitions, like having a certain pen to play Bingo with, using a series of personally significant numbers, including birth, wedding or anniversary dates and lucky house numbers, or putting your clothes on in a certain order when you wake up in the morning. What appears to be a simple quirk can affect us in a dire and often dangerous way, and by taking on a ritual we can influence curses and turn them into blessings, exchange negatives and create positives and influence the dark negatives of life in exchange for the assured Providence of God.

There are those who state that they are not influenced by superstitious beliefs, but it may be worth remembering that not being superstitious is in itself a superstition. Some superstitions are traceable, but the vast majority of the origins are lost in the mists of time.

In Nottinghamshire there are some superstitions found almost exclusively in the area. One in particular relates to imperfections found upon a woman – a mole on the neck, for instance, denotes that there is wealth in store for her, A local rhyme, quoted exclusively in the county of Nottingham, is as follows:

> *I have a mole above my right eye,*
> *And shall be a lady before I day;*
> *As things may happen, as things may fall,*
> *Who knows but that I may be Lady of Bunny Hall?*

According to another version, of which there are several, we are reminded that:

> *If a Nottingham maiden bears a mole above her chin,*
> *She'll never be beholden to any of her kin.*

In Newark members of the Young Farmers' Club used to carry a plough into Newark Parish Church for a Sunday service, after which it was blessed in the hope that it would bring prosperity to the farming community and ensure fertile crops.

A local newspaper clipping records the following Nottinghamshire superstition: 'An old plough was blessed at East Bridgford parish church last night to mark the annual Plough Sunday service and distribution of charity bread. . .The service marked an old tradition when ploughboys took a plough round village farms and performed small plays for which they received tips.'

Many people believe that quirks of nature, such as a flower blooming at the wrong time of year or a comet passing through our skies, foretell events that are yet to come, normally being of a disastrous nature.

If you have a look at the older farm houses in the county you will see that trees such as holly and yew have been planted beside the doors. This was carried out in the hope that evil and bad luck would be averted. The holly and yew are prime examples of trees that were believed to have magical powers. Both symbolise long life and prosperity.

Apple trees were once viewed as being very lucky, and those maidens of Nottinghamshire who wanted to find a husband were advised to go to an apple tree on Christmas morning or New Year's day and allow the sunshine to fall upon them. This, apparently, would bring luck and love to the maidens as well as indicating a bumper crop of apples in the forthcoming year. If there was no sunshine then it foretold of a barren year ahead, both in love and apple production.

The following are some examples of the many superstitions that are associated with the natural world:

Ant – An ant found climbing up your arm indicates news is on its way. A red ant is important and interesting news and a black ant is bad news. A black ant found climbing up your left arm indicates you will shortly be attending a funeral.

Bats – If bats are seen to fly in a circular motion after sunset, it is believed that fair and warm weather is on the way. A bat in the house is an indication of very good news, and to own a dead bat is said to bring prosperity. In some parts of the world, especially Asia Minor, carrying bat bones in your purse means that you will never be short of money.

Cat – The cat has always been associated with witches and the secrets of the afterlife. Cats are said to be 'half in, half out', which means that their souls exist half in heaven and half in hell, and they walk the line between good and bad. In Nottinghamshire it is generally accepted that a black cat brings good luck if seen on your right side, while bad luck is certain if seen on your left. To see a black cat directly cross your path, regardless of whether it is on your left or right, is considered to be extremely lucky.

Dog – To hear a dog howling at night or to meet a black dog on commencing a journey is a sign of bad luck. According to gypsy law, it is incredibly unlucky if a dog digs a hole in your garden. If a strange dog follows you it is a sign of good luck, which will occur very soon.

Fork – Dropping a fork is considered lucky, indicating that a woman will visit bearing good news.

Goat – It is believed by many to be one of the forms in which Satan can appear. An old legend tells how goats are never seen for 24 hours continuously as they have to appear in Hell for Satan to comb their beards.

Hare – This animal was once killed by the Romans, who used its entrails to divine the future, but the animal was rarely eaten. To see a hare means much luck and happiness is to come.

Handkerchief – Tying a knot in a handkerchief to remember something symbolises a very ancient belief that the knot is a universal charm against bad luck and the evil eye. Demons and witches were said to be intrigued by the shape of the knot and all thoughts of bringing misfortune to you would go from their minds.

Hat – Placing your hat on a table will bring misfortune, while putting your hat on back to front will bring good luck. Wearing a hat in a building is a sure sign of bad luck about to descend, and to spit in your hat was to avert any form of bad luck.

Lamb – If the first lamb of the season that you see has its head facing towards you, it is a sign of bad luck for the forthcoming year, especially if you are carrying money on your person.

Magpie – Often referred to as the Devil's Bird, many people consider it to be an bad omen. To avert any misfortune, it might be wise to whisper this ancient charm: 'I cross one magpie, one magpie crosses me. May the devil take the magpie and God take me.'

Peacock – The feathers of a peacock are thought to be extremely unlucky, and to have them in the house is even worse.

Rook – Rooks, ravens and other members of the Corvidae family are said to carry the souls of the dead to heaven. These creatures were once worshipped and attributed with magical powers of perception. Should the ravens at the Tower of London ever fly away, it is said the country will plunge into ruin. This tale is similar to the legend that surrounds the rooks at Newstead Abbey.

Rabbit – Carrying the foot of a rabbit was once believed to be lucky. Miners in Nottinghamshire are said to be very superstitious about the rabbit because if you see one near a mine entrance it means there will be an accident.

Shoes – To place a new pair of shoes on a table will bring very bad luck to their owners. To place a silver coin in a bride's shoe denotes a successful and happy marriage.

Toad – Should a bride encounter a toad on her wedding day, it means it will be a prosperous and fertile marriage.

George's Lane, Calverton

If you happen to be travelling in your car along the long and winding George's Lane at Calverton on a dark and lonely night, try to refrain from glancing too much in your rear view mirror, as you might encounter the face of an old grim lady with a glint of malice in her eye. No one knows who the old lady is, but legend says she was murdered in the vicinity. Others claim that she is the spirit of a suicide who threw herself under a car.

Ministry of Angels.

Supernature

The Realm of the Fairies

'Elementals' are said to be lesser evolved spiritual entities, although some schools of thought maintain that in many ways they are more evolved than human souls. According to some spiritual belief systems, there is a whole range of spiritual entities that exist above and below human spirituality, and the world of spirits is far more complicated than originally thought. Our ancient ancestors living in the Nottinghamshire area were undoubtedly animistic in their belief systems. Animism is the belief that everything has a soul, spirit and a life force that requires respect. It is the belief that everything from rocks, trees, water and flowers to the dirt has a spirit – a living entity within it – and that all things are spiritually animated. Our ancient ancestors practised Nature spirit worship, and some people believe that Robin Hood is a reference to the sacred Father of the Wood who protected the trees and plants that thrived within the forests.

There are very few places in Nottinghamshire that do not have stories of spirits or entities associated with them, haunting the woodlands, green fields, caves, rivers and lonesome stretches of water. These strange ghosts are said to be apparitions who have never existed in human form, and occultists claim they are ancient spirits ruled by higher spiritual powers known by titles such as the Mighty Ones. Elementals are said to pre-date man and fall into four categories: Earth, Air, Fire and Water.

The Realm of Earth

There have been recent sightings of earth elementals, sometimes known collectively as gnomes, in the grounds of Wollaton Hall. A group of children claim to have seen a number of these creatures riding around in mysterious and odd-shaped vehicles. These mysterious elementals are said to be the protectors of lost or hidden treasures, which they keep deep within caves beneath the earth. Brownies are another example of earth-loving spirits. They are small, wear brown clothing and attach themselves to certain families, and could prove useful in menial household tasks. However, if you have a troublesome Brownie you need to leave it a small piece of wearable clothing, like a cloak or a hat, and they will leave and never trouble you again.

The Realm of Air

These elusive spirits are said to have the ability to cause storms and bring about heavy winds, causing damage to property. They often take the human form of an old haggard woman and can speak the language of birds. These spirits have the ability to fly and are said to be the most evolved of the fae, and there have been reports of such a creature being seen at Creswell Crags recently. These immortal creatures are said to be trapped in the space between dimensions.

The Realm of Fire

Fire is a natural element that our ancestors believed was a life-giving force. These entities are collectively known as salamanders and are said to be temperamental spirits. There have been many reports of small balls of light and fire dancing and swirling around in marshy areas of Nottinghamshire – a possible sighting of these salamanders? They have been known

as the Will o' the Wisp, Corpse Candle and Jack O' Lantern, and in Europe they are known as Ignus Fatuus (Foolish Fire). In Nottinghamshire they have become known as Earth Lights.

Just across the border, Derbyshire is said to have more recorded sightings of these strange fire spirits than anywhere else in the world, while in Nottinghamshire there are dozens of reports of strange lights being seen in the fields and lonesome places, especially in autumn and at dusk, just after the sun has set. Many believe that we each have a salamander within us throughout life, helping us to maintain body temperature and circulation.

The Realm of Water

Often referred to as undines or ondines, these beings can be found within any body of water, from the oceans, rivers and the largest lakes to the smallest rock pool. They are said to be dressed in shiny attire and their clothes change colour, mimicking the shimmer of the water they inhabit. These creatures of supernatural origin live across Nottinghamshire, in nearly every wood, coppice and forest, and if you can catch one it is said to bring either great luck or disaster, but if you harm one it will bring ruination and an everlasting curse to your bloodline.

The Black Dog of Beckingham

> For he was speechless, ghastly, wan,
> Like him of whom the story ran,
> Who spoke the spectre hound in man.
> Sir Walter Scott, *The lay of the last minstrel*, Canto VI, v.26.

Sightings of phantom black dogs are numerous throughout Britain, and virtually every area has its own variant. Barguest, Shriker, Guytrash, Black Shuck and Hell Hounds are a just a few names given to such apparitions. Various gods associated with the underworld, hunting, birth

Dog has been man's best friend since the dawn of civilisation, but dogs are also said to be portents of doom and disaster. According to ancient superstitious beliefs dogs also watch over sacred sites and holy places.

and death are also connected with these dogs, such as Hecate, Diana and Artemis. There is also the story of Gabriel Ratchet's hounds, which are said to race across the night skies chasing human souls condemned to hell for eternity. Black dogs seem to haunt ancient lanes, crossroads, areas of woodland and churchyards.

According to A.D. Mills's *A Dictionary of English Place-Names*, the small village of Beckingham's name comes from the Old English Becca+inga+ham, or 'homestead of the family or followers of Bassa', and is of Anglo-Saxon origin. Before the present-day bypass, there existed a main road which ran from Sheffield to Gainsborough through the heart of Beckingham village, and villagers once reported seeing an enormous black dog that would run quietly along it. The beast was reported to have stood as tall as a man's shoulder and had huge glowing eyes that seemed to burn with the fires of hell itself. This otherworldly dog has been seen emerging from the local cemetery, moving quietly but with purpose, continuing along the old road and turning off towards the old boatyard, crossing the water meadows beside the River Trent and heading off in a southerly direction before vanishing from sight.

One local is said to have confronted the beast one dark night. Standing in front of the infernal creature he raised his hand and demanded to know, in God's name, what the creature's business was. But no sooner had he spoken the words than he was struck by a paralysis, which left him lying unconscious in the middle of the road. Some time later he was found mumbling incoherently. He never recovered from his ghostly experience and, according to local legend, spent the rest of his days completely paralysed down one side of his body.

It is said, and believed by many, that the black dog of Beckingham was once the guardian beast of a local Lord of the Manor. In the early seventh century, when Christianity was first brought to Nottinghamshire, the local Lord of the Manor was a Pagan and refused to even consider the concept and doctrine of the Christian faith. So adamant was he not to convert that he trained his trusty guard dog to attack any Christian trespassers that came onto his property. One day the missionary priest visited the lord, but instead of the dog attacking him it lay down and gave itself over to being petted and fussed. When the priest left, the dog followed him; the two were inseparable, and the dog would go about the countryside converting Pagans with his new master. Some time after, the dog died and the priest buried it in the churchyard, and from that time to this day the dog is said to guard the churchyard against evil. It is thought that Satan himself would not set hoof there for fear of the phantom dog.

One of the first mentionings of these phantom creatures comes from the *Anglo-Saxon Chronicle*, dated 1127:

Let no one be surprised at the truth of what we are about to relate, for it was common knowledge throughout the whole country that immediately after his arrival [Abbot Henry of Poitou at Abbey of Peterborough] – it was the Sunday when they sing Exurge Quare o, D – many men both saw and heard a great number of huntsmen hunting. The huntsmen were black, huge and hideous, and rode on black horses and on black he-goats and their hounds were jet black with eyes like saucers and horrible. This was seen in the very deer park of the town of Peterborough and in all the woods that stretch from that same town to Stamford, and in the night the monks heard them sounding and winding their horns. Reliable witnesses who kept watch in the night declared that there might well have been as many as twenty or thirty of them winding their horns as near they could tell. This was seen and heard from the time of his arrival all through Lent and right up to Easter.

Other tales of ghostly black dogs abound in Nottinghamshire, including a document dating back to 1952 in Nottingham County Library that records the words of Mrs Smalley, who was then about 75 years old. She recalls a story concerning her grandfather (born in 1804). He would often drive from Southwell to Bathley in his pony and trap, and the journey involved going along Crow Lane, which leaves South Muskham and leads to Bathley. On numerous occasions he saw a black dog running alongside his trap. In 1915 his great-grandson, Mrs Smalley's son Sidney, owned a motorcycle and would often go into Newark to the local dance and would return home late, at about 11 o'clock at night. He, too, frequently saw a black dog in Crow Lane; on occasion he would try to run over it without success. Confounded by what exactly this black dog was, he decided to ride out with his father on the back of the motorcycle to see if they could both see the creature, and sure enough as they rode along Crow Lane the beast appeared running alongside them.

In yet another part of Nottinghamshire, this time near Worksop, close to Hodsock Priory, a young woman was driving home late one night when a large black dog with red eyes appeared in the middle of the road. She described the dog as like no other she had ever seen before. With short, shiny skin and upright ears it was very large in size and was dragging something large across the road. She was relieved when the beast finally moved on, and she was able to continue her journey. Later she was to discover that close to where she had seen the creature were ancient burial mounds. Could this animal have been an ancient protector of the site, like so many other British legends state?

The Origins of Christmas

Christmas is one of the busiest times of the year. It lasts for only a few weeks and yet there are so many customs and practices that we have to remember and observe. When studying all these customs, it soon becomes clear that the origins of many of them go further back than we could possibly imagine. The following is an attempt to look at a number of of those customs, some of them being universal and a few particular to Nottinghamshire.

Mummers Day

The most unique Nottinghamshire Christmas folklore practice is that of Plough Monday, or Plough Bullocks, Plough Day Fair, Epiphany Fair or, as it is more widely known, Mummers Day. This one-day festival usually took place during December or January and involved actors known as hoodeners travelling from village to village to perform a play in fancy dress. Some people believe that it was performed to drive out any evil spirits present in the village, as recorded in the *Newark Advertiser* on 18 January 1871. The ancient custom consisted of the following:

> *A party of mummers visited the towns and villages of North Notts during the past fortnight and highly diverted the inhabitants by their dancing, singing of old songs, and the play of the Hobby Horse.*

The play was in existence in the days of the Plantagenets, and probably the song and tune that they sang was *When Joan's ale was new*.

Another form of the play was performed on the second Monday in January. In this version Tom Fool was the narrator, and a three-way operatic scene between a recruiting sergeant, a farmer's man and a lady followed. In the scene the farmer's man joins the army, so the lady decides to marry the fool. The next scene includes an Old Dame, usually called Jane, and Beelzebub, or Eezum Squeezum, which ends up with Dame Jane being violently knocked to the floor. A doctor is then summoned to perform an elaborate comical cure, and the whole play ends up in a song. The play has strong similarities to modern day pantomime.

Advent Wreath

The origins of the Advent wreath are found in the folk practices of the pre-Christian Germanic peoples, who, during the cold December darkness of Eastern Europe, gathered wreaths of evergreen and lit fires as signs of hope. This practice was also carried out in order to placate their pagan gods and appease the spirits of nature by offering them shelter for the winter.

Traditionally, the wreath is made of four candles placed in a circle of evergreens. Three candles are violet or blue (blue symbolising the hope of the season and the violet representing penance, as in Lent), and the fourth is rose-coloured, but four white, violet, blue or red candles can also be used.

Christmas Eve

It was once believed that on the stroke of midnight farm animals acquired the miraculous and unusual gift of speech. Oxen, cows, horses, pigs, and poultry began to speak to one another and to exchange strange secrets about humans, particularly their masters. However, bad luck, the risk of being struck dumb or, worse still, even death came to those who tried to spy on them. Another belief says that at midnight farm cattle kneel in the stable to worship the infant Jesus. It is clear that these two beliefs are closely linked to the even older one that Jesus was born at midnight

Predicting the Future

On Christmas Eve, young girls would resort to certain customs to try to discover the name, or at least the initials, of their future husbands. Nottinghamshire girls would write the letters of the alphabet on pieces of virgin white parchment and place the pieces of paper face down into a bucket of water, which they would then place near or under their beds. In the morning they would check the bucket and if they were lucky, or unlucky depending on what the bucket of letters foretold, they would find the name of their future husband spelled out by the letters that had turned over during the night.

The Christmas Nativity is a scene we are all familiar with, but the origins of Christmas go back much further than the advent of Christ.

Origins

Before Christianity, there were many pagan religious festivals around 25 December. The best known were those of Saturnalia, from December 17 to 24, the cult of Mithras, which is celebrated on 25 December, and the festival of the Sigillaria at the end of December.

The festival of the Sigillaria, or terracotta seals, was a pagan Roman holiday. At the end of Saturnalia Romans used to give gifts, especially to children, such as rings, seals and tiny objects. This festival was the time for great feasts, during which houses were decorated with green plants.

Hanging Stockings

The custom of hanging stockings originates in England. It was once said that Father Christmas dropped some gold coins while coming down the chimney. The coins would have fallen through the ash grate and been lost if they hadn't landed in a stocking that had been hung out to dry, so children have continued to hang out stockings in the hope of finding them filled with gifts.

The hanging of stockings by the fire supposedly dates back to the actual Saint Nicholas, a bishop in Lycia in Asia Minor (present-day Turkey) during the fourth century AD. According to the legend, there was a poor man with three daughters who could not provide a dowry for them to be married. One night, Nicholas secretly dropped a bag of gold into an open window of the house. The oldest daughter was then allowed to be married. This was repeated later with the second daughter. Finally, determined to uncover his benefactor, the father secretly hid each evening by his daughter's window, until he caught the saint tossing in a bag of gold. Nicholas begged the man not to reveal what he had done; however, word

There was once a widespread belief that on Christmas Eve the dead rise from the grave to pay homage to the cross.

got out anyway, and whenever anyone received a gift from an unknown source it was attributed to Saint Nicholas.

Greenery

The hanging of greenery around the house, such as holly and ivy, is a winter tradition with origins dating back well before the Christian era. Greenery was once brought into the house to lift sagging winter spirits and remind people that spring was not far away. The needle-like points of holly leaves are thought by some to resemble the crown of thorns that Jesus wore when he was crucified. The red berries symbolise the drops of blood he shed.

Mistletoe, also known in Nottinghamshire as kiss and tell and in other areas as thunder blossom, is found on willow and apple trees (and occasionally oak). The practice of hanging it in the house goes back to the times of the ancient Druids. It is supposed to possess mystical powers that bring good luck to the household and ward off evil spirits.

Christmas Tree

The fir tree has a long association with Christianity. It began in Germany almost 1,000 years ago when St Boniface, who converted the German people to Christianity, was said to have come across a group of pagans about to sacrifice a young boy while worshipping an oak tree. In anger, St Boniface is said to have cut down the oak tree, and to his amazement a young fir tree sprang up from the roots of the oak tree. St Boniface took this as a sign of the Christian faith. It was not until the 16th century that fir trees were brought indoors at Christmas time. The decorating of Christmas trees, though primarily a German custom, has been widely popular in England since 1841 when Prince Albert had a Christmas tree set up in Windsor Castle for Queen Victoria and their children.

The Yule Log

The Yule log was originally an entire tree, carefully chosen and brought into the house with great ceremony. The large end would be placed into the hearth, while the rest of the tree stuck out into the room. The log would be lit from the remains of the previous year's log, which had been carefully stored away and slowly fed into the fire through the 12 days of festivities. Having the remains of the Yule log in the house throughout the year was thought to give protection against fire, and it was considered important that the re-lighting process was carried out with clean hands. Nowadays, of course, most people have central heating so it is very difficult to burn a tree! However, the Yule Log has been replaced in our modern day homes by a much more appetising version – that of the chocolate yule log.

Christmas Crackers

The idea of the cracker was conceived in 1850 by a London confectioner called Tom Smith, who, while sitting in front of his log fire, found his concentration interrupted by the sounds of sparks and crackles emanating from the fire. He thought what an added attraction it would be if his sweets and toys could be revealed with a crack and a pop when their fancy wrappings were pulled off. Today's crackers are short cardboard tubes wrapped in colourful paper and traditionally we have one cracker next to each plate on the Christmas dinner table. When the crackers are pulled, out falls a colourful party hat, a toy or gift and a festive joke. The party hats found in Christmas crackers look like crowns and we assume symbolise those worn by the three kings.

Christmas Pudding

Over the years many superstitions have surrounded this popular festive dessert. It is said that puddings should be made by the 25th Sunday after Trinity, prepared with 13 ingredients to represent Christ and his disciples; every member of the family must take turns to stir the pudding with a wooden spoon from east to west, in honour of the three kings.

Putting a silver coin in the pudding is another age-old custom that is said to bring wealth, health and happiness to whoever finds it. Other items put in the mixture over the years include rings, which indicate marriage within a year, and thimbles and buttons – which predict the finders will remain spinsters and bachelors.

Life before life? Reincarnation

In the beginning, before the time of man, there existed in the universe beings which were androgynous. These beings were without need as we know it; being totally at one with themselves, they needed no other stimuli to exist. Being both able to reproduce by themselves and having no determined length of time in which to exist and die, they subsisted in total bliss. The Gods in that time watched the creatures closely and eventually became envious of their total completeness. Becoming angered by these beings' unique oneness, the Gods split them in two, cast them down to this world, bound them in flesh and, from that day to this, those beings – us – seek to find that which we were divided from. Forever seeking our other halves, forever asking ourselves when we meet potential partners, 'Is this the one?' When we eventually find that which we were divided from, we will become whole again, thus allowing ourselves to pass on to a spiritual dimension where we may once again exist in total bliss.

So reads one of the many legends associated with reincarnation. Although this may be a simple way of looking at the subject – and admittedly rather a romantic one – the reality of reincarnation and what it means is a great deal more complex, surrounded by much mystery, argument and debate.

Throughout the world belief in reincarnation appears to be growing. Our ancient Celtic ancestors dwelling in Nottinghamshire would almost certainly have believed in the often religious doctrine that the souls of humans, as well as animals, had the ability to transmigrate,

at the point of death, from one biological form to be reborn in another. It was believed in ancient Celtic mythology that the corpses of slain warriors were cast into a cauldron of rebirth, from which they arose refreshed and ready once again to do battle with their enemies. These beliefs were likely to have been held by the ancient people of Nottinghamshire. Indeed, throughout the world, in nearly all spiritual and religious backgrounds (especially Hinduism and Buddhism), we find the belief in continuous life cycles common.

In Christianity the belief in reincarnation was a strong one until the sixth century when the Emperor Justinian issued 15 'anathemas' – formal ecclesiastical curses involving

Hypnosis is said to be able to unlock the partition of the mind that blocks out our previous lifetimes.

excommunication – which condemned the idea of reincarnation. The Christian church appears to have deplored the idea ever since, even though they believe their prophet and son of God, Jesus of Nazareth, himself rose from the dead.

Seven signs that someone has been reincarnated

- Remembering things you know you have never personally experienced.
- Being drawn to a specific period in history, which you seem to know more about than any other.
- Vivid dreams of events, music, food and people you have no recollection of meeting.
- Fears and anxieties about everyday items and places, such as knives, fire, water, swords, horses or machinery, with no rational reason to explain why these items or places upset or unnerve you.
- Strange bodily marks or wounds that you have no conscious recollection of happening.
- Understanding another culture, including the language, people and idiosyncrasies.
- As a child, feeling that your name is incorrect and calling yourself by a different one.

Many modern hypnotherapists claim to have the ability to access previous lives through a series of suggestive phrases and words which soothe the conscious mind – allowing a doorway to our past lives to be opened. In this semi-conscious state, we are sometimes allowed to glimpse images of lives past. Many books abound in the market concerning alleged regressed individuals who claim to have verified their past lives through intensive and thorough historical research.

Most people, at some time or another, have experienced the strange feeling of déjà vu, which is a feeling of having already experienced the present situation, such as knowing what to expect further along a country road not journeyed before. These types of occurrence are not uncommon and there are several theories as to why these feelings of familiarity happen to many people on a frequent basis.

Scientists claim that the human mind is capable of convincing us that we are experiencing memories from a past lifetime, when what we are actually perceiving is only a regurgitation of an article or book, or other visual stimulation we have experienced years, or even decades before. This process, known as cryptomnesia (remembering things once forgotten), is currently under investigation and research in universities and medical centres throughout the world.

However, the mystical and spiritually inclined accept the concept of reincarnation, claiming that we are continuously reborn as part of a spiritual learning process. When we have learned all that is necessary to have advanced our souls to a state of reasonable divine purity, we can at last pass on to another higher level of spirituality for ever.

Feast for the Dead

Those who have taken their own lives are said to return to the place where they committed suicide, there to lament their unhappy and eternal damnation, on Hallowe'en.

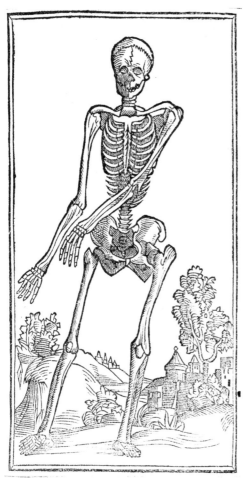

There was a time when the very mention of All Hallows Eve struck terror into men and women. Nottinghamshire's ancient dwellers had no doubt that elves, pixies, fairies, goblins and demons existed, or that the dead walked the earth. Special services were once held by the Christian church at this time of year to bless its congregation in a bid to keep evil forces at bay. Bells were rung throughout towns and villages, and holy water was sprinkled on the doorsteps of houses.

Now, most people view the annual celebration with little or no fear at all. Hallowe'en is, to most of us, a time of merriment and fun; a time for children to dress in ghoulish costumes and knock on doors, trick-or-treating, with a look of expectation on their faces. The practice of dressing up in costumes is not an entirely new concept, however, it derives from an ancient practice when man believed that to dress in such a way would enable them to go unnoticed by evil forces out to do harm. Nevertheless, how many of those fun-seeking youngsters realise that the true origins of Hallowe'en are both sinister and complex?

To many Pagans 31 October is Samhain and is a particularly important time of the year, when the two worlds — those of the living and the dead — are thought to be near each other. There are four great Sabbaths and four lesser Sabbaths, referred to as Escatts, in the Pagan year. Hallowe'en is perhaps the

most important. This time of year also marked the end of summer and the beginning of winter. The ancient Celts only recognised those two seasons. Huge bonfires would be lit on hillsides across England and the spirits of the dead were encouraged to find their way back to this world.

Contrary to popular belief Hallowe'en was, in fact, never a sombre or grim occasion to Pagans but a time of cheerful merriment, remembrance and goodwill – a time to honour and worship the dead. Music, dancing and loud celebrations took place. In addition, candles were once placed in windows to guide the souls of the departed back home, and this practice is still common in many parts of the British Isles. Another ancient practice was to leave food and wine on the table and a fire in the hearth before retiring to bed, as these offerings to the dead would surely bring favourable fortune to the household throughout the forthcoming year.

Finally, for those who carve faces in pumpkins to place on dark windowsills, it is worth remembering that this was once done to attract the spirits of the dead. The grim faces were carved in an attempt to ward off evil spirits, while the flames that burned within the pumpkins were intended to light the way. Beware…!

The Magic of Hallowe'en

Love Apple Charm

At midnight, take a large red apple and peel it with a black-handled knife so that the peel forms one continuous coil, then stand facing a large mirror in a room lit by the flame of a virgin white candle. Holding the peel in the left hand (the hand traditionally said to be linked directly to the heart), turn three times then cast the peel over the right shoulder. Behold! The skin will fall to the floor, forming the initials of your true love. Should the skin break into many pieces, the outlook is considered to be gloomy. A word of warning – do not look into the mirror after the peel has been thrown, as you may see reflected there a face that is not of this world. This charm can also be used at Christmas to predict the future.

Pumpkins, the grotesque faces carved upon pumpkins was originally an attempt to ward off evil spirits, while the light that burned within was intended to light the way for the souls of the departed back to earth, thus allowing us to celebrate those whom we have lost.

The Clay Charm

Take four pieces of white paper, and write the names of three admirers in blood-red ink on three of them. Roll the pieces of paper into small balls and encase them within wet clay. Place the clay balls in a bowl of water into which you have first added a handful of salt, then place the bowl underneath or near to your bed.

In the morning, one of the clay balls should have released its contents – the name written on the floating piece of paper is believed to be the name of the lover that you will marry. Should the blank piece of paper be the only one floating then you are yet to meet your true love.

A similar charm involves writing the letters of the alphabet on small pieces of cardboard before placing them face down into a bucket of water. In the morning, check to see which pieces have turned over during the night, and these letters are thought to spell the name of your true love.

Evil Eye Charm

For those who still believe in the evil eye, think that they may have been cursed or just want to change their luck for the better, the following charm is believed to promote good fortune and keep evil away.

On the evening of Hallowe'en take an egg, the shell of which should be as light as possible – white being the best – and draw on it the universal antidote against evil – the Cross. Next, carefully carry the egg into the garden and deposit it into a shallow grave. Spit into the hole and rapidly fill it in, then walk away and forget about it. Your luck is sure to change for the better.

The Apple Twig Charm

According to some, this next charm is a very potent one. Before midnight has struck on All Hallows Eve, take a black-handled knife and go to an apple tree. From the tree, cut three short twigs; should you be able to collect mistletoe this is even better and adds to the potency. Next, tie the twigs or mistletoe with red thread wrapped three times about them, and then place them under your bed. Take a candle and stick three pins into it while repeating this charm:

'It's not the candle alone I stick

But my would-be lover's heart I prick;

Be he asleep or be he awake,

A vision of him this night I call to make.'

Burn the candle for an hour then extinguish the flame. Within the next three nights you should dream of the one you will marry.

Haunted Trees

'Under the greenwood tree

Who loves to lie with me

And tune his merry note

Unto the sweet bird's throat

Come hither, come hither, come hither

Here shall he see no enemy

But winter and rough weather.'

William Shakespeare

Lone Tree. Enigmatic trees found standing alone have long had the reputation of being places where ancient spirits dwell. Tying votive pieces of cloth on to such trees is said to inspire the tree spirit to grant a wish to the individual.

Trees have always played an important part in world religions. References include the Bo tree, under which the great Buddha sat, the spectacular Yggdrasil of Norse mythology, upon which the god Odin hung and spied the runes, the barren fig tree that Jesus of Nazareth cursed and, of course, the elder tree upon which Judas later hanged himself.

The Druids were said to worship trees and were known as the keepers of the old religion. Their temples were the sacred oak groves, and they believed that all things in creation harboured the spirits of their dead ancestors as well as elemental spirits of nature. The very word 'Druid' is said to translate into 'knowing the oak tree'. The main trees the Druids worshipped were the oak, apple, rowan, willow, ash, beech and birch. These Celtic beliefs were at one time so widely believed that the Council of Tours in 567 declared that those who 'worshipped trees, stones or fountains' should be excommunicated.

Today there is very little left of the ancient groves and mystical trees that once scattered the face of Nottinghamshire, apart from a few random trees which have at some point been said to be haunted by phantoms, spirits of nature and the 'little people' of folklore and legend.

Trees were once sacred to Pagans and Druids, who showed certain trees great respect by including them in their ceremonies.

Trees have been worshipped and respected since the beginning of mankind. Today farmers will often leave a single tree standing in the middle of a field for fear of upsetting the spirit that dwells within.

Nottinghamshire's most famous tree is undoubtedly the major oak in Sherwood Forest. This giant tree, with a waistline of 35ft, a height of 52ft and an estimated weight of an astonishing 23 tons, is thought to have been growing for 800–1,100 years. The exact age of this magnificent tree can only be roughly estimated, and the answer probably lies in the magnitude of its size; however, it has been known for some oak trees to grow faster then others. The tree has a large canopy, and the leaves and branches have a spread of 92ft, which suggests that the tree has grown up with little or no competition from other oaks nearby, thus allowing the large branches and network of leaves to spread out.

The major oak's first recorded name was the Cockpen tree, which referred to its earlier use as a cockerel pen during the mid-18th century. These cruelly-treated game birds were stacked inside the tree in baskets or thrust up in hessian sacking. Eventually they were released and pitilessly thrown together for this archaic and cruel sport.

The oak is said to be haunted by Robin Hood himself. According to legend this was the tree in which Robin Hood hid from the Sheriff of Nottingham's men when they were in active pursuit of him. In recent years several people have claimed to have seen a man dressed in green in close proximity to the tree. Other strange happenings have occurred near the tree, including unusual balls of light seen dancing about in the upper branches, and a strange groaning noise that the tree is said to make can be heard at certain times of the year.

Another tree with a legendary connection to Robin Hood is the Doveridge yew, just across the border with Derbyshire, under whose branches Robin Hood and Maid Marian were said to have been married; the ghost of a green man is also frequently seen here.

Granny Knows Best

In books and manuscripts there are numerous references to cures that seem strange and bizarre by today's standards. It seems that many of the cures are surrounded by elements of magic and mysticism. Perhaps this is because man, in his inconsistent knowledge,

sought the help of ancient spirits of healing to bring about a better cure. Perhaps it was ignorance, or could it just be that the ancient soothsayers and healers knew more than we credit them for?

In many parts of Nottinghamshire it was not uncommon to find such items as animal skulls and even painted eyes placed above doors and windows of houses in a bid to avert the evil eye. Several discoveries of 'witch jars' (bottles filled with pins, broken glass, roots and herbs) in the Nottingham area have been unearthed in the foundations of old houses, a definite indication of the widespread belief in magic in the past. Archaeological finds of human and animal skulls in the River Trent, which have clearly been placed there and are not a result of suicide or accidental death, suggest that ancient man was placing the skulls in the river, perhaps in order to placate the spirits of the water or in relation to some magical cure. These skulls might account for the many ghosts that have been sighted on, in and near to the river.

When people fell ill, there was often no alternative but to visit a wise man or woman. Most villages had one, although with the onslaught of witch hunts and persecution trials of anyone vaguely associated with magic, local healers and sages went underground and became rare.

Nevertheless, the practice of going to see a healer continued. Anything could be treated – from head lice to the plague. There was a cure for nearly everything and, if the herbs and potions failed, it was often blamed on black magic.

When the Black Death raged throughout England in 1665, there sprang up a whole series of strange and peculiar healing remedies. Some of the things used to cure plague included common vegetables, tomatoes, fruits, nettles, Juniper berries, pigs fat and eating live frogs. The people living at the time viewed such cures as very possible and considering the circumstances probably their best hope. Another strange cure for the plague was based on warm beer, which would be infused herbs which had been picked at an exact astrological moment. All herbs and plants were at one time assigned to an astrological planet.

In the village of East Stoke near Newark the parish records for 1646 reveal that there were 161 burials that year, of which 159 were as a result of the plague that was ravaging England. At that time some people believed that it was caused by God, who infected sinners with the disease as a punishment for their crimes. Just a mile away in Syerston, also served by the same priest, the death toll for the year was just two, and the records reveal that marriages were significantly above average – 15 in that year. Perhaps the locals believed that a God-fearing way of life, including marriage, was the cure for the terrible plague?

Urine seemed to be one of the most frequently used granny cures. Stale or fresh, urine was thought to be all-healing, having at some point been used to treat most exterior conditions and, on occasion, internal ones. One Nottingham cure mentions pouring warm urine into the ear to cure an infection. Another mentions tying an old smelly sock around your wrist to draw out fever.

Then there was the crucifix, which was used as an external antidote against most illnesses. The practice of carrying a crucifix or cross was often not just for religious or pious purposes. It was commonly believed that illnesses were brought about by little demons that entered the body, making the person ill.

Herbs appear to play the greatest part in cures. Today's homeopathic cures are nearly all based on earlier discoveries. Modern medicine also owes much to ancient granny cures; indeed, many drugs are directly derived from the same herbs they used in the past.

Vampires – Folklore or Fact?

Rising from their cold, dark graves to suck the blood of mortals, vampires kill indiscriminately and care little for human emotions. There was a time when such creatures were believed to wander the face of the earth, seeking to destroy all human life. Today the debate continues: do vampires exist or not?

There are those who believe they are living vampires and those who study and discuss vampire fiction and folklore. For decades, folklorists and vampirologists have been busy studying the universal spread of the vampire – every culture has a vampire of its own. Vampires are identified in every aspect of mythic and folklore. There are undead vampires, living, psychic or supernatural vampires, vampire deities, demons, spirits and animals. Ghouls, gods, succubi (demons that sleep with humans), psychopaths, devils and witches are all crowded under the same heading. They are all vampires, but for different reasons.

When living people call themselves real vampires and attempt to define what they mean by the word, they are usually unable to do so with clarity. Real vampires may be blood drinkers or psychic vampires, they may be twisted or borné, and they may have any combination of secondary traits or none at all. Depending on which source you read, real vampires may be inheritors, classical, viral or just 'wannabes'. Ultimately the definition of a vampire seems to be open to interpretation. Above all, they are a mystery.

We are most familiar with what Hollywood has portrayed as the dark classic vampire, and we have grown to love them and hate them at the same time. But research shows that

Vampires fear anything with a Christian origin. Crucifixes, holy water and Bibles are just some of the objects said to repel these unholy creatures.

the dark classic vampire is nothing more than a collection of inspired, attention-grabbing creations and a betrayal of what vampires really are.

Nottingham has numerous stories of these creatures stalking in the shadows in search of victims, and some say the reason vagrants are scarce in the county is because of the presence of vampires, including the strange sighting of a large winged creature flying over the Market Square.

The Black Death struck the town in 1349, and one of the symptoms of the plague was a coma or deep sleep. With so many people dying, it was quite common for people who were still alive to be brought out to the funerary collector and taken directly to their place of burial. However, there were several reports of people being buried alive and frantically trying to claw their way out of their coffins. These incidents gave rise to speculation that the plague was sent by Satan and that these poor unfortunates were vampires – the dead rising. Because of the vast number of plague victims, space for burials began to run out, so people were buried on the outskirts of town. Certain parts of Nottingham and the county became out of bounds after darkness for fear of meeting something otherworldly. Today the vampire legend still continues to fascinate people.

Spirits of Nature

There are many local legends of people seeing strange creatures – ghosts, goblins, fairies, water spirits and so on – in Nottinghamshire. For generations, people have believed that such creatures exist and to disturb or upset one of them, by cutting down a sacred tree or building a wall across an ancient fairy dell, would inevitably bring about ruin. Farmers were especially wary of nature spirits and would often plant holly, rowan or thorn trees, which were believed to have magical powers and would protect the house from these mischievous spirits.

Today we may scoff at the idea of a spirit residing in a tree, a cave, a stretch of water or a well, but to ancient man residing in the valleys and forests of Nottinghamshire, these

Fauns are said to be the protectors of the woodlands, forests and glades. At midnight the spirits of the trees (Dryads) are said to make themselves visible and dance and hold high jubilee with other nature spirits.

creatures of antiquity and nature were very real. Many people believe that the Green Man legend (Robin Hood) – a representation of an ancient fertility god representing the cycle of death to the birth of new life – is entirely indigenous to Nottinghamshire when, in fact, there are reports of him in nearly all the counties in the East Midlands.

As the peoples of our country rapidly became Christianised, they adapted older beliefs into the new doctrine. Not content to entirely let go of the old ways, they incorporated many of their mythical figures into the fabric of their churches. We need only to look at many of our present-day churches that have survived from the 14th, 15th and 16th centuries to see that the people who designed and built them still partly believed in the Celtic gods and spirits.

Many churches still have an abundance of carved stone heads. Green Men are normally shown with leaves coming out of their mouths, and the image can be found, usually carved from stone, high on cathedral and church buildings that date as far back as the 11th century. Sheela-na-Gigs (goddesses of fertility) can also be found within Nottinghamshire; one particular excellent example is a carving at Southwell Minster. Other various stone carvings such as gargoyles, horned men, mouth pullers, tongue stickers and strange animals are all perhaps representations of forgotten gods and goddesses.

Our ancestors also knew the value of clean water; it is rumoured that they often sacrificed a young virgin to placate the earth gods and goddesses. Many serious investigators of the paranormal have pondered why there seem to be so many reported incidents of white ladies

haunting the countryside and ancient places; perhaps this is because of the sacrificed virgins who are bound by Druid magic to protect the place that they gave up their lives for.

Most wells and waterways are thought to be haunted, and in many parts of England it was common, at certain times of the year, for locals to make special trips to certain stretches of water to drink from them, believing that the water was imbued with miraculous healing powers. These beliefs, once again, appear to descend from our ancestors, who made comparisons between natural phenomena in nature and human anatomy. Certain rivers and water stretches are known to change colour, from yellow ochre to brown and red, when there has been heavy rainfall and flooding. Superstitious people often believed that the changing water colour was a sign of a magical transformation, which the spirits of the water, or the gods, were allowing to happen for fertility purposes. So a river turning red from flooding water running through a clay bed was often thought to represent the fact that a god had allowed its own blood to mingle with the water, thus reinforcing the life-giving qualities of the water with the god's own life force. Others believed that the river turning reddish or brown was an indication of the Earth Mother (or Goddess of Nature) menstruating, while others believed it to be an omen of misfortune and an indication that those who were once sacrificed to the waters were reminding all of their presence.

Forbidden Worlds

Stockinger's Rest – Cauldwell Dam

A Watcher by the Water

The gruesome history of Cauldwell Dam, near Sutton-in-Ashfield and Mansfield, goes back a very long way. Over the past few centuries numerous suicides have taken place there, some of them under very suspicious circumstances.

On more than one occasion, visitors to the dam have reported seeing what appears to be a young woman dressed in unusual attire. Some say she wears Victorian costume, others say she is wearing tattered rags and still others have described her as wearing modern dress. She is always seen sitting at the edge of the water, often with her head in her hands crying, and when approached by concerned onlookers she simply vanishes.

Having heard several versions of encounters with this ghostly apparition, I am of the opinion that we may be dealing with several ghosts. Cauldwell Dam is also known as 'Stockinger's Rest' – a name taken from an earlier time when Sutton was one of a series of small villages that harboured a prolific cottage industry, namely that of making exquisite, as well as functional, stockings for the wealthy. According to records the first hand-frames for making such garments was introduced sometime around the mid-18th century and were installed into homes to produce the much sought-after hosiery products. The cottage industry continued to thrive, but the slow advance of technology combined with capitalist merchants' underhanded greed was to have a devastating effect on the industry.

In 1811 the Luddite Movement came into existence. Luddism is a name, according to legend, which derived from one Ned Ludd who, having been told to work faster by his master and then having been reported to the local magistrate who ordered him to be flogged, picked up a hammer and demolished his weaving frame.

Eventually factories were built to house new modern machinery that increased garment production and cut down on the number of employees needed, and when steam-powered machines were installed this devastated what little of the cottage industry was left. Hundreds, possibly thousands, of families fell into deep poverty and were unable to cope; many relocated to different areas and attempted to get alternative employment. The local parish council had to take care of the desolate, sick, bewildered and those with mental health problems. Unable to cope with the numbers of unemployed homeless, poor unfortunates were confined to workhouses; a name which, even today, strikes fear and dread into many a steadfast heart. Workhouses were notoriously tough places to live in, with harsh regimes and tough conditions. To enter into a workhouse was seen as a complete and utter failure, so faced with no employment and the prospect of going into a workhouse, many of the former stocking makers decided to take their own lives. Records reveal that numerous suicides took place at Cauldwell Dam, and further research has revealed that other deaths have occurred, usually listed under 'drowning accident'. In 1900 two teenagers committed suicide together by drowning themselves – a pact they had entered into? A murder? A suicide? No one can say for sure.

Who knows what dark determined thoughts ran through the minds of the men and women that took their final journey along the hedge-lined Cauldwell Road before finally plunging themselves into the dark icy waters of the dam and launching themselves into eternity forever?

The Watcher in the Water

It was the summer of 1930, and Enid Harrison was 14 years old when she encountered the apparition of a crying girl on the banks of Cauldwell Dam. She had gone there with her boyfriend Harry, for what she describes as 'precious time together'. Harry was four years older than Enid, and her parents had forbidden her to see him.

They were happily enjoying the summer afternoon and had decided to sit among the wild flowers and the undergrowth, chatting about anything and everything, as sweethearts often do. She explained:

Harry was eating an apple. He was teasing me with it and holding it above my head just out of my reach. We were laughing when suddenly, from just behind us, we both heard the sound of someone crying. It was the distinct sound of a woman's voice! Harry immediately jumped up and went to investigate. 'Stay here,' he said, and I just did as I was told. There was something about the crying, it was pitiful, unhappy and even when I think of it now I get an uncomfortable prickly feeling running up my spine. Harry vanished into some nearby trees and as he did so the crying altered and instead of coming from the direction of where he had headed off to, it was coming from the opposite direction near the water's edge. I waited for Harry to come back, but after a minute he still hadn't, so I decided to investigate myself. I edged tentatively towards the water's edge which must have been about 15 feet away from me, it in turn dropped down steeply to the shoreline. As I came closer I could see a young woman dressed in a blue cotton dress sitting at the water's edge, she was soaking wet and I could see the water dripping from her hair and clothes. Concerned I moved towards her and asked if she was ok, she didn't reply, she just simply continued to sit there gazing out onto the water and sobbing. There was something about her, something wrong; something deeply unhappy about her countenance, it was horrible and I never want to feel that sensation again. I turned around to see if I could see Harry, he was heading towards me, smiling as he usually did. When I looked back at the crying woman, she was gone! I immediately went to where she had been sitting and looked into the water, but the water was perfectly still, she couldn't have jumped in. The strange thing was that the grass where she had been sitting was bone dry, I even touched the spot and there wasn't a drop of moisture in an area I knew had to be saturated with the wet from where, moments before, the crying woman had been seated! I immediately told Harry what had happened and he just laughed at me, in fact he laughed at me for the next few weeks, constantly reminding me about my ghostly encounter. I've been back there on several occasions since. I stand on the exact same spot and look for her. I know she is there because I can feel her watching me. I feel so completely alone and unhappy when I stand on that spot. I call to her and ask her to let me see her. She has never appeared again. She doesn't speak, she doesn't have to. I think a long time ago she was a jilted lover who in desperation took her own life.

The Language of Flowers

There was a time when man looked deeper into the meaning of all things that inhabited and grew upon the earth, and it was from the dawn of civilisation that man began to give particular attention to flowers. Their beauty must have stirred the imagination, eventually giving way to flowers being endowed and credited with magical and curative powers. Eventually, folklore naturally became interwoven with superstition, which in turn caused a vast amount of literature and legend to appear on the subject. This interest has continued to grow and there are now hundreds of books dedicated to the subject on the shelves of bookshops.

Flowers have many given meanings and over the centuries we have given certain flowers to one another in order to convey specific messages. They have been wreathed round the new-born baby's cradle, are carried by the bride and adorn the marriage altar, are sent to an admirer and are also left on graves.

It has been alleged (although it has not been proved) that the Black Death inspired one of England's most famous nursery rhymes, Ring-a-ring o' roses. The 'Ring around a rosie' supposedly referred to the red rash, the first symptom of the disease. 'Ashes, ashes' or

'Atishoo, Atishoo' referred to the sneezing sound made by the person infected, and the last line of the rhyme, 'We all fall down' represented the many deaths resulting from the disease.

Perhaps the most interesting line of this rhyme is the second, 'A pocket full of Posies', which refers to the practice of carrying flowers in the belief that it would protect the infected person. Some flowers are still said to hold protective powers for those who carry or grow them. For example, some say that to carry a sprig of yarrow will provide protection from any negative forces, while others say that you

The Language of Flowers. Lilly of the Valley is a common grave flower and represents eternal love and heavenly blessings.

must carry a sachet of peony flowers if you feel you are victim of the 'evil eye'. There is also a belief that the foxglove, traditionally known as the 'flower of sorcery', will keep away all evil spirits.

In Victorian times, the subject of flower lore became extremely popular. Mediums of the day took to using the subject of flowers as a practical means of divining the future. This practice has continued to the present day and there are still those who claim the ability to divine future events from a flower or leaf an inquirer might pick. Indeed, whole services have been dedicated to the use of reading flowers and plants. Individuals wanting to make contact with a dead relative or know of some future element in their lives need only pick or chose a flower. They would even take it along to a service and place it on a tray, normally where the medium cannot see it, and later have it analysed. At this point, the medium will try to discover which person picked or chose the flower.

The Language of Flowers. Death carvings. Carvings of flowers and fruit on gravestones can be found all over the world. Flowers took on a language of their own. Daffodils, seen here, represent spring and innocence.

This may appear to be a dubious way of making contact with the spirit world, yet there are those who state they have witnessed astoundingly accurate results.

The Victorians also sent flowers as a means of communication. However, it was of utmost importance that those involved believed in the same meanings as many flower dictionaries of the time contradicted each other, therefore causing many misunderstandings and arguments.

The following list of flowers, their divinatory and superstitious meanings, is perhaps one of the more common lists of interpretations to be found. For those wishing to study this ancient art, it is worth remembering that it is equally important to give the flower a

Where a white foxglove grows no evil may enter that house. A white foxglove signifies that the house is protected by the fairies.

meaning that is also apparent to you because to divine a flowers meaning by inner intuition is just as good as knowing and using its ancient interpretation.

Acorn or oak leaf – A symbol of long life and immortality which is now representative of Nottinghamshire as the Major Oak at Sherwood Forest is an icon of the shire.

Anemone – Sickness, forsaken and forlornness.

Angelica – Inspiration and protection, also known as the flower of the angels.

Apple – Protection and fertility, honesty and virtue.

Bachelor's Button – Love and marriage.

Basil – Best wishes, love, kindness and constancy.

Bay Leaf - Strength and fortitude.

Buttercup – Ungratefulness and conceit. The smell was once thought to cause insanity.

Bluebell – Some say tragic loss, others state it is the flower of constant kindness.

Carnation – Said to have sprung from the tears of the Virgin Mary on her way to Calvary. A lucky flower.

Camomile – Hope in a hopeless situation.

Calendula (Marigold) – Joy, hope and everlasting life.

Chrysanthemums – Love, truth and happiness.

Crocus – Youthful hope, an end of a troubled time.

Daffodil – Regard and chivalry. To find the first bloom growing denotes a year when you will have more gold than silver.

Dahlia – Instability and illness.

Daisy – Flower of the children. Innocence and sentiment.

Dandelion – Courage and strength.

Dead leaves – Sadness, melancholy and a funeral.

Fern – Sincerity.

Forget-Me-Not – True love remembered.

Foxglove – Keeps away evil spirits and was traditionally known as the flower of sorcery.

Garlic – Courage; strength, protection against evil.

Geranium – Stupidity and folly, also the flower of treachery.

Goldenrod – Health, encouragement and good fortune.

Grass – Submission. Failure.

Hollyhock – The flower of fruitfulness.

Honeysuckle – New love and friendship.

Hyacinth – Said to have sprung from the blood of a friend slain by the god Apollo. A flower of regeneration.

Iris – A message travels towards you. Guidance.

Ivy – New friends and acquaintances.

Jasmine – Grace and elegance. Divided love reunited.

Jonquil – I want you to love me.

Lavender – Long life. According to one legend, the lavender once did not have any scent. The Virgin Mary hung the clothes of the infant Jesus on the bush to dry, and from that day to this, the plant has been imbued with its magical scent. This legend gave rise to the ancient belief that lavender flowers keep away evil spirits.

Lilac – Unlucky to have in the house as it attracts spirits, a flower of humility.

Lily – Purity and sweetness. Folklore states that lilies, unplanted by human hand, would spontaneously appear on the graves of people executed for crimes they did not commit. It is also said that the use of lilies at funerals symbolises the restored innocence of the soul at death.

Lily of the Valley – The return of happiness.

Love in a Mist – Love at first sight.

Magnolia – A love of all things in nature.

Mint – Protection from illness; warmth and well-being.

Narcissus – Vanity and egotism.

Orange blossom – Chastity and purity. News of a wedding.

Pansy – Once considered an extremely magical plant. William Shakespeare confirmed its magical uses when he wrote how Oberon squeezed juice from the flower of the pansy into Titania's eyes as she slept, so that, when she awoke she would fall in love with the first person she saw.

Peony – The seeds were once used to place curses on people. The flower of shame.
Poppy – Remembrance and consolation.
Primrose – A new life awaits you.
Rhododendron – Caution, you are moving into danger.
Rose – Love and beauty.
Shamrock – Laughter and cheer, goodwill and blessings.
Snapdragon – Presumption.
Snowdrops – Another flower which is said to have sprung from the tears of the Virgin Mary. A flower of kindness.
Sunflower – Adoration and pride.
Thistle – False friends and enemies.
Tuberose – Dangerous pleasures.
Tulip – Fame and fortune.
Violet – Faithfulness in love.
Wildflower – Fidelity in misfortune.

Saints Among Us

There was a time when man not only prayed to God but also to an array of saints who, if moved by the individual's pious request in prayer, would intervene and grant whatever the plea might be or at least bring out an alternative, satisfactory solution to the problem.

The word saint, as we have come to understand it, is more widely used in the Christian sense, especially within the Catholic faith. Saints were given their canonised titles by popes, whereas Celtic saints achieved their grand titles by the popular veneration of the people of the day, much to the annoyance of the later Catholic Church.

God in the highest heaven bestowed special gifts and abilities on those that showed particular homage and servitude to the greater good of mankind.

By praying to specific saints it was believed that the saint would take intermediate action between God and man, thus helping the request within the prayer to be granted or answered more quickly.

Holy men and women have always played an important part in western religions, from pre-Christian times until the present day, although today they are not as widely idolised as they once were. Most saints were people who, after death, were formally recognised, especially by the Roman Catholic Church, as having attained by holy deeds while alive great veneration by the poor and desolate people of their time. They often led lives of total devotion to their faith and were frequently purported to heal the sick and the dying, as well as performing other remarkable miracles.

Specific saints dealt with specific requests, so if a saint had died in childbirth (Saint Margaret) then ladies suffering from any health problems concerning pregnancy or childbirth would pray to her asking for help and intervention in the matter. Within the Catholic church, votive candles are still burned to invoke the favour of the requested saint, and it is further believed by many that, in most cases, the saint's intervention between man and God gets the answer and solution that is needed. The following list is a brief guide to some of the more frequently invoked saints and what patronage they represent:

St George – Patron Saint of England and for all those fighting a battle. (AD303)

St Sebastian – Patron saint against plague and pestilence. (AD288)

St Roch – Patron saint of those who languish in prison or who are trapped. (AD27)

St Cosmo and St Damian – Patron saints of medicine. (AD301)

St Gertrude of Nivelles – Patron saint of the fear of mice. (AD656)

St Isidore of Seville – Patron Saint of the Internet. (Seventh century)

St Rene Goupil – Patron Saint of Anaesthesiologists. (17th century)

St Barbara – Patron saint of explosions, including thunder and lightning. (AD303)

St Hubert of Liege – Patron Saint of mad dogs. (Eighth century)

St Phocas – Patron saint of gardens and gardeners. (AD303)

St Pantelion – Patron saint of physicians. (Fourth century)

St Apollonia – Patroness against toothache and all diseases of the mouth. (AD250)

St Cecilia – Patroness of music and musicians. (AD280)

St Agatha – Patroness against all diseases of the breast and of fire. (AD251)

St Fiacre – Patron Saint of sexually transmitted diseases. (Seventh century)

St Alexis – Patron saint of pilgrims and beggars. (AD400)

St Blaise – Patron saint of diseases of the throat and of wild animals. (AD289)

St Martin – Patron saint of penitent drunkards. (AD397)

St Eloy – Patron saint of goldsmiths, locksmiths and blacksmiths. (AD659)

St Anthony – Patron saint of anything lost. (AD357)

St Leonard – Patron saint of prisoners, captives and slaves. (AD559)

St Zita – Patron Saint of domestic workers, maids and lost keys. (AD1278)

Rufford Abbey

The county park of Rufford Abbey is situated two miles south of Ollerton and 17 miles north of Nottingham, near to the A614 Nottingham road. The native forests of oak, lime and birch were probably originally cleared by Neolithic people; the whole area has ancient remnants of human occupation from the earliest of times. The Romans arrived around AD120, records reveal that there was a settlement near Runford, and it is very likely that a Roman road would have passed through the area from Oxton to Blythe, situated in the north.

The first recorded owner of Rumford or Rugforde was a Saxon man named Ulf, but after the Norman Conquest William I gained the estate and gave it to his nephew, Gilbert de Grant, for his loyalty. By the early 12th century the stone construction of Rufford Abbey was well underway, although it is thought that work may well have continued for more then a century. Local stonemasons, joiners and other artisans were hired to construct the abbey, and many of the materials were sourced locally.

Life at the abbey for the Cistercian monks was not easy. They would have had to work hard and pray hard in order to stay within the religious order. After a year at the abbey they would take their vow of silence, and novices then received the famous tonsure haircut – a central bald patch on the top of their head – and a black scapular apron and leather belt.

Rufford Abbey. A ghostly black monk is reputed to haunt the abbey.

They gave up all their possessions and vowed to obey the abbott at all times. Many of the educated monks devoted their time to prayer and meditation. Some copied out books within the scriptorium, a special writing room, and used their creative skills to illuminate manuscripts with gold leaf and beautiful embellished colours. Most of the less educated monks would have worked the fields and gardens, which amply provided the abbey with vegetables (the Cistercian order was vegetarian), wood for fires and even fabric. All seemed well at the abbey until Henry VIII broke away from the doctrine of Rome.

Prior to 1536 Henry had ordered Thomas Cromwell, his vicar-general, to carry out an audit of all the monasteries. It was completed within six months, resulting in some very wrong decisions. Cromwell, who had his own agenda, reported: 'Manifest sin, vicious, carnal and abominable living is daily used and committed among the little and small abbeys.' With greed at the forefront of their motivations, Cromwell's audit laid charges against certain abbeys concerning debauchery, bestiality, homosexuality and Satanism, to name a few. At Rufford it was alleged that the abbey possessed some of the Virgin Mary's milk, and further allegations were made about Abbott Thomas of Doncaster, claiming that he had broken his vows of chastity with at least six women – two married and four single. Six other monks were also accused of being of 'disgraceful character'.

In 1537 the abbey and its lands were granted to George Talbot, 4th Earl of Shrewsbury, and it was to remain in the family for some time. Rufford passed through the centuries virtually unscathed, and different owners and families that lived in the building only added to its beauty.

By the early 20th century the Rufford estate comprised over 18,500 acres, but had begun to feel the effects of increasing running costs and falling incomes from the farms and cottages it owned. It was eventually sold in 1938, and the estate at that time included 2,000 acres of woodland, 500 acres of deer park, several public houses and numerous domestic properties in the surrounding villages. Most of the land was purchased by Sir Albert Ball, a Nottinghamshire industrialist, who resold the country house and its grounds to the eccentric Henry de Vere Clifton. By the late 1940s the main buildings were suffering from structural damage.

Today the remains of Rufford Abbey and all the park buildings are a Grade II listed ancient monument. A very popular country park and top Nottinghamshire tourist attraction, it receives over half a million visitors per year. And it is no wonder, with such a long and ancient history, that the abbey buildings and surrounding land are said to be one of the most haunted sites in Nottinghamshire. Ghostly reports of phantom black dogs, hooded monks and white, blue and green ladies circulate. Local legend talks of a Black Friar who may be seen on moonlit nights wandering the grounds. He is also said to approach onlookers and, while standing directly in front of them, pulls back his cowl to reveal not an ashen ghostly face but a grinning skull. Shortly afterwards it is believed the onlooker is doomed to die, just as one gentleman did after encountering the friar in the winter of 1901. Other tales tell of the Black Friar riding through the grounds on a phantom coach and horses, his

The unhappy spirit of Lady Arabella Stuart haunts Rufford Abbey. Her ghost may be seen wandering close to the house, and her ghostly presence is accompanied by the beautiful smell of roses.

bony white skeleton and grinning skull seen through his ragged garments as he mercilessly whips the horses to go faster.

Other spirits not at rest include Lady Arabella Stuart, who was born at the abbey in 1575 and spent a happy childhood there. She was the daughter of Elizabeth Cavendish and Charles Lennox, who was the brother of Lord Darnley, the late husband of Mary, Queen of Scots, which made Arabella a major claimant to both the English and Scottish thrones, having both Tudor and Stuart bloodlines. Queen Elizabeth feared for Arabella's choice in lovers and sent her to live with her grandmother, the Countess of Shrewsbury (Bess of Hardwick), who was to keep her safe from deceitful noblemen.

When James VI of Scotland succeeded Elizabeth I to the English throne, becoming James I of England, he brought Arabella to London to keep an eye on her activities. He clearly wasn't watching her closely enough, as she secretly married William Seymour, son of the Earl of Hertford, on 22 June 1610 at Greenwich. There was a major panic, due mainly to the fact that Arabella and her new husband were direct descendants of both of the sisters of Henry VIII. No doubt King James I viewed their marriage as a real threat to the throne.

The two were imprisoned, and both plotted their escapes successfully. Arabella dressed as a young man and made her way to France, where she was to meet with her husband. However, she was arrested by the king's men at Calais and brought back to England, being imprisoned in a luxury section of the Tower of London. She died there on 27 September 1615 of self-starvation and, some say, a broken heart.

Arabella's ghostly figure may still be seen at Rufford, wandering the area close to the house. She is oblivious to any passers-by and even when approached continues walking in a hasty fashion back to the house. She is believed to be accompanied by the smell of roses, and some say she has been seen crying and always looks sad and dejected, but this is no surprise when you consider her tragic circumstances, for she was the Queen of England that never was!

More ghosts reported at Rufford include a man hanging from a tree, a small frowning girl who points at the house and runs away, strange lights and mists seen emanating from the area of the ice houses, a screaming woman and a phantom nanny seen pushing a pushchair. Who these ghosts are and why they haunt the area is not yet known.

Wraith of Shades

Interpreting Orbs:

The New Wave of Spirit Photography

At the end of the 20th century reports of strange, often colourful, ghostly orbs caught on camera began to emerge from all over the world. Stories soon began to circulate that these orbs were the captured images of spirits. This new form of 'spirit photography' coincided with the advent of phone cameras and new digital photography techniques, which were being eagerly embraced by a hungry market of creatively adventurous people. People were delighted that they could digitally take a picture and print it from their computer within minutes of it being taken. Gone were the traditional days of sending away your roll of film and waiting a week or two before the pictures were processed at a lab, returned and then collected.

For centuries mystics had claimed to be able to see auras and spirits, which they further claimed would appear to them in the form of spherical lights of differing sizes, densities and colours. Was this absolute proof that spirits did actually exist and could even be photographed? Maybe, but no one has the answer. For those that believe no explanation is needed, and for those that do not, no amount of proof will ever be enough. So what are these strange orbs found on digital pictures? Flecks of dust perhaps trapped on the lens? Minute particles of metals suspended in the atmosphere of a room that, when photographed with a digital camera, reflect light in such a way as to appear like an orb of light? Or are they survivors of the dead appearing on increasingly sensitive technology? One thing is for sure, this new wave of spirit photography is here to stay – until it can be finally explained one way or the other.

The following colours and their meanings are what psychics and mystics use to decipher the meaning of orbs and auras that they see around people. The colour is an indication of what the spirit was like in personality when they were alive. Likewise, the colours that often appear in blotches around people in photographs are an indication of their temperament and personality or, at the very least, are a clue to their mood at the time the picture was taken.

Red

Red is the colour of energy, passion, anger and love (depending on density). The best colour to be found in an orb or the aura is rose red, the colour of universal love and inner beauty.

Yellow

Yellow is the colour of the intellectual and of clear thought processes. Orbs that display yellow are said to have been optimistic, pleasant people who had a balanced outlook on life in general, although their intellectual capacities in life were often under-stimulated if the colour dominates the orb or aura.

Blue

The colour of peace and beauty is blue. Deep blue within the aura or an orb can indicate a strong emotional constitution and is said to indicate stability as well as long life. Blue is also the colour of healing. Electric blue will indicate spiritual awareness and latent psychic ability; mediums and psychics are often said to display this colour within their auras.

Violet

Violet is the colour of the highest vibration of light. It is said to be stimulating and is the colour of creativity and spirituality. It is not the colour for the masses but is found more often in the auras of spiritually-developed individuals who care little or none for material possessions. Guardian angels are said to appear as a violet orb.

Silver

The colour silver shows energy and a strong will, and orbs with this colour are said to have been adventurous in life and would have sampled all aspects of living. People with this colour in their aura are often 'ideas people'.

Grey

When found in the aura, grey will indicate illness, mental depression and a lack of sensitivity. When found in an orb, it is an indication that this spirit was once an ignorant, calculated and crude individual with an inability to adjust to life's ever-changing pattern.

Orange

The colour orange indicates vitality; or lack of it if the colour is found to be dark and murky. This colour often appears in the aura when the individual is in the process of recovery, be it spiritually, mentally or emotionally. When in an orb, it is an indication of an individual who was optimistic, kind, energetic and understanding.

Green

Harmony and balance; nursing and nurturing and care and kindness are manifest in the colour green, in the aura and as an orb. Green will also indicate an individual's ability to communicate, but a dark and dirty green is an indication of an evil disposition; people and orbs who display this colour cannot be trusted.

Indigo

Indigo is often the colour of nervous energy and mental and psychic forces, although too much of this colour within the aura indicates a highly suggestive and neurotic personality that is given to outbursts of uncontrollable self-pity. Orbs who have this colour are spirits who are believed to have been kind, good listeners and often took on the role of counselling.

Gold

Gold indicates a materialistic attitude towards life when found predominating the aura or an orb; although in small amounts, gold will indicate a lack of self-esteem and a giving nature.

White

The colour white represents purity, goodness, kindness and compassion. Buddha's aura was said to be pure white and extended itself over one mile. Angels and further-evolved entities manifest themselves as white orbs.

Of course, it gets really complicated when an orb contains several or even all of the colours, as you have to interpret the colours by the degree of shade, size and intensity.

Things That Go Bark in the Night

Since earliest times, man has revered certain species of animals for many reasons; some for their ability to live in harmony with humans, to love and in turn be loved, appreciated and cared for, and some for their innate ability to see the future.

Perhaps it is for these reasons — as well as for companionship and an obvious food source — that man decided to welcome all manner of creatures into the warmth of his home.

Many nations have worshipped animals, often in half-human form, as their gods and supernatural guardians; especially in Ancient Egypt where all manner of creatures were worshipped, from the majestic lion to the fearsome jackal, humble beetle and bee. So revered were certain animals that, when they died, several weeks were often taken up in elaborate mourning and ceremonial embalming procedures before the creature was finally entombed amid much pomp and ceremony.

Native American Indians were familiar with animal telepathy; they believed they could communicate with all manner of creatures, especially wolves, which found great honour in the Indian totem. They gleaned much information from the wolves and watched their behaviour to define the weather.

Anubis, the Egyptian God of the Dead. In ancient Egypt dogs were once worshipped in the form of the canine jackal. The dog in folklore is the guardian of the departed, protecting the deceased and their last resting places from evil.

Over recent years much research has gone into understanding the link between humans and their pets. One scientist has dedicated a whole lifetime to the study of animal telepathy and, in investigating over 900 cases, one doctor claims to have discovered a definite link, which he describes as an invisible and 'morphic field', that exists between hundreds and thousands of pets and their owners.

For many years it has been believed that bees are telepathic and have a strong sense of what is happening to their keeper's family. It is common practice for beekeepers to inform the hive of any major events such as births, marriages and deaths, because if the bees are not told they will feel betrayed and abandon the hive. Bees are so in tune with their owners' lives that they are believed to attend their beekeeper's funeral.

The bond between pet and owner is said to be so strong that when something happens to one, the other immediately senses it. For many people this will not seem unusual or bizarre; stories of telepathic occurrences are often told by ordinary, down-to-earth people who have no axe to grind on the subject whatsoever. Many people are familiar with the feeling that their pets often know exactly what they are thinking, and some owners have pets which sit by the telephone shortly before it rings, often with important news. One lady states that she used to ask her dog whether she should put her washing on the line or not, as she believed the dog could predict the weather; if the dog ran to the door, she could assume that the weather would remain fine, but if he remained where he was, she knew that the weather was going to take a turn for the worse and her washing would be rained upon.

Animals are also said to sense stress in their owners and relieve it by the process of being stroked. National magazines have often produced articles which claim that stroking our household pets not only relieves stress and anxiety but is good for our health in general.

Witches were said to be able to shapeshift and take on the appearance of a black dog, hare or wolf. These creatures were in past times persecuted because of such beliefs.

But why are animals so telepathic? Perhaps it is that we are so advanced with technology and modern conditioning that we have forgotten how to use areas of our brains which most creatures, great and small, are still in touch with and continue to use. This phenomenon has now become known as Low Frequency Telepathy (LFT).

Holy Wells

St Catherine's Well (Southwell)

St Catherine's Well is one of the few remaining holy wells around Southwell, even though it lies in the adjoining village of Westhorpe. Dating back to the mediaeval times, its waters were once said to be able to heal rheumatism as well as other bone and muscle conditions. In the 1700s there was an attempt to turn the well into a spa.

Robin Hood's Well (Beauvale)

The sacred waters of Robin Hood's Well were once believed to be an aphrodisiac. The water supplied a nearby Carthusian priory, so this is probably where it got its reputation as a holy well. There once stood a temple on the site, but there is nothing to be seen of it today, as it has been razed to the ground.

St Mary's Well (Newstead)

St Mary's Well is located at the head of a pool just behind Newstead Abbey, and it is said to have generalised healing powers. In the past this well would have served as a source of water for the main house.

St Ann's Well (Nottingham)

Situated about two miles north-east of Nottingham, St Ann's Well is believed to have been in existence as early as 1280. Its first name is recorded as Owswell, but from 1500 it was commonly known as 'Robin Hood's Well', due to a reputed affray that occurred there involving Robin Hood and his merry men. By the end of the 18th century the well had gained a reputation for being healing: 'The water is very old. It will kill a toad. It is used by those who are afflicted with rheumatic pains.'

During the 19th century the adjoining area was known to be a less desirable place to live as the residents were believed to be rowdy; a pub on the site was closed down for unsociable behaviour and noise. Later the building became a tea room. Most of the buildings in the area were demolished in 1887 to make way for a railway line; at this point the well was lost for nearly a century, and in 1987 it was rediscovered in a public house car park in Wells Road.

Headless Phantoms

Whatever stories abound concerning headless phantoms, the whole of the British Isles is strewn with tales of these decapitated wraiths. Several writers specialising in the supernatural have suggested that the primary reason for so many headless ghosts is perhaps due to the fact that it was once relatively common practice to decapitate the dead – this was done in the belief that it would put a stop to any spirits of warriors who were slain by Celtic head-hunters. Another school of thought maintains that these wraiths are the result of so many people being beheaded, from mediaeval times onwards, for political crimes against the monarchy. Archaeological excavations of numerous Pagan, Celtic and Saxon burials have revealed that many of the remains of the interred corpses had been removed, and the skulls were then placed between the knees or the feet.

Many of the headless phantoms that haunt the dark recesses of our world are male, although some can materialise as women, dogs and horses. Various ghosts either carry their dismembered heads under their arms, or are completely headless, and the rare one or two have their heads placed on backwards.

Every shire in the country appears to have their own individual headless phantoms. Many are seen on moonlit nights riding headless horses, while others are seen meandering through our valleys and villages in horse-drawn carriages, often carrying an empty coffin, which is believed to be for the unfortunate individual who meets the gruesome cortège.

Many of the reported headless phantoms are male, although some can materialise as women, dogs and horses. These supernatural visitors either carry their dismembered heads under their arms or are completely without a head.

As to where the missing heads from these decapitated phantoms are, many of our shires have been abundant in screaming skulls at some point. These curios, which for centuries have been known to reside in many of our farms or, more often than not, our manor houses, are thought to be a by-product of the headless phantoms. Being notoriously spooky artefacts, these recalcitrant objects have been known to wreak havoc and mayhem if they are in any way moved or upset. Many famous accounts exist of screaming skulls being moved or thrown out of properties, only to be reinstated in their original positions. When the skulls have been removed, it is often common to hear that disaster befell the residents shortly afterwards. Farm animals often come down with mysterious diseases while the owner, or even the individual responsible for the cleansing, is dogged by exceptionally bad luck or mishap.

Other areas of the world have equally interesting stories to tell of headless phantoms and ancient skulls. Perhaps the most famous accounts of strange skulls are the ones said to have originally come from mysterious temples deep within the Mexican rain forests. These skulls, said to total 12, are carved from solid quartz crystal and are believed by many to have magical qualities. According to the legend, when the skulls are placed together it will signify the end of the world. In recent times, television programmes have been dedicated to the subject, and the final findings concluded that the skulls were indeed of ancient origin, and much of the workmanship which created the skulls is remarkable, considering they were alleged to have been created by such rustic people.

Shiver and Shake

Gargoyles

The word 'gargoyle' comes from the Latin 'gurgulio' and the Old French 'gargouille'. Both words not only mean throat, but also relate to the gurgling sound made by the rainwater as it runs through the gargoyle figure.

Gargoyles are carvings on the outside of buildings originally designed as a drainage system to direct water away from the walls, thus preventing damage and deterioration. Some of the earliest-known forms can be traced back to the time of the ancient Greeks, when they were fashioned out of terracotta. Later, wooden carvings emerged before carvings of stone became popular, reaching the height of fashion in the Gothic period. As time progressed, more and more imaginatively-decorated carvings appeared, including representations of animals, beasts and demonic spirits, as well as people, many of which were humorous and referred to as 'grotesques'. After the introduction of the lead drainpipe in the 16th century, gargoyles primarily served a decorative function.

Superstition held that gargoyles frightened away evil spirits, as well as carrying out their practical function. Many parishioners believed that the gargoyles adorning their church not only warded off evil spirits, keeping purity within their place of worship, but also acted as a reminder of the perils of evil; hopefully encouraging the non-believers to change their ways and join them for worship.

Many of these grotesquely-carved figures adorn churches across Nottinghamshire. Whole legends have sprung up concerning certain gargoyles; perhaps it is no small coincidence that these same stories have direct relevance to the fact that the churches stand on ancient Pagan sites adopted by the Christian church.

Superstition held that gargoyles frightened away evil spirits, as well as carrying out their practical function of removing rain water from the church building.

The more hideous the gargoyle, the more potent it would be in averting evil spirits intent on causing good Christians harm. Some gargoyles are said to come alive and stalk the churchyard at dawn and dusk.

Touched by an Angel

The 'Great Chain of Being' is a classical western mediaeval conception of the order of the universe; a somewhat complicated hierarchical system composing of numerous links from the most basic elements – the rocks and the earth – to the highest perfection at the top of the chain – God. Everything has its own assigned place within the chain, giving order and meaning to the universe. Directly beneath God in the chain are the angels, who are subdivided into their own ranks: archangels, seraphim, cherubim, thrones and several others. It is said that there are seven angels that stand before the throne of God: Gabriel, Fanuel, Michael, Uriel, Raphael, Israel and Uzziel.

It seems that man has always believed in the existence of angelic beings that mediate between the realms of mortals and the immortal gods, bearing messages of great spiritual importance, guiding the hand of man and silently watching in the wings. Only in recent times it would appear that angels are physically and more frequently changing the fate of certain desperate and needy individuals.

In the Judeo-Christian culture the word 'angels' signifies their work as messengers, other words denote their essence. To many, these celestial beings are known as sons of God,

Angels are said to answer prayers and through angelic intervention our lives are believed to be guided. Many people believe that they know when their guardian angel is with them when they discover a white feather.

ministers, servants, watchers or the holy ones. To others, they are known as spirits and heavenly hosts. In Psalms they are referred to as 'the chariots of God', while in the book of Job they are called 'morning stars'. Ancient references to angels describe them as wingless, residing close to man; so close in fact that the sons of God had intercourse with the beautiful 'daughters of men', producing a race of people known as Nephilim. It was only later, in 600BC, that angels and archangels appeared to move to a higher spiritual sphere, seemingly too pure by this time to reside so close to mankind.

Most Westerners, when they hear the word 'angel', automatically think of Christianity, and the images they describe are reminiscent of the depiction of angels in Christian art; beautiful, winged human forms. Many believe that angels are entirely of Christian or Judaic origin. In truth, angels are encountered in Hinduism, Shamanism, Buddhism, Taoism, Zoroastrianism

Many people claim that they have a guardian angel that watches over them, intervening only when they are truly needed. Some individuals claim to have had their lives saved by such heavenly creatures.

The Great Chain of Being.

and Islam, among others. Angels were also frequently found in Paganism; you only have to look at mediaeval churches to see thinly-disguised Pagan gods in the form of angels: Hermes, Victory, Earth Mother, Eros, Pan and many more.

Modern-day individuals who study angels (angelologists) insist that we would not recognise an angel even if we stood next to one. They also believe that angels and other such supernatural spiritual custodians are drawn to an individual through need and not want. Many people claim that we all have a guardian angel that watches over us, intervening only when we need them to, often without us realising it. Many also believe that they have had their lives saved by such heavenly creatures.

Such supernatural occurrences are not as uncommon as we might imagine. Indeed, all across Nottinghamshire, reports of angelic intervention in ordinary people's lives are on the increase: a stranger who helps an old lady across a busy road, the woman with medical knowledge who happens to be present when a man has a heart attack, the man who helps at the scene of a roadside accident before vanishing into the crowd and any stranger who just happens to appear at the exact moment when help is needed. All these individuals, of natural or supernatural origin, can be deemed angels. As to any real evidence of their existence, we have only the mysterious messages that occasionally appear in the personal columns of newspapers, thanking a stranger who has helped another in distress. These communications are perhaps the only signs that angels leave behind. We can explain away most other claims of angelic manifestations as natural occurrences, but not all. Indeed, many sightings may be due to over-active imaginations, others caused by sheer tiredness, while some may even be mild hallucinations caused by a myriad of different things. There still remain, however, those which we cannot explain.

There is a current belief that angels manifest themselves to us in the form of white feathers, which mysteriously appear when we least expect to see them. There are accounts of people comforted by the discovery of a feather, believing it to show that their guardian angel is with them.

The Future in a Cup

Throughout history there have always been thousands of people who have claimed the ability to see the future. Prophesy appears to have always existed, even though those who claimed the ability were often hunted, persecuted and put to death, often because those in power feared their abilities. Tea leaf reading, or tasseography, has been used for thousands of years by novices and learned mystics to lift the misty veils of time and allow the questioner to glance into the future. In order to become masterful in the art of tea leaf reading, one must allow the imagination freedom to interpret the images that the conscious eye sees. We have all, at some time, seen faces on the living room carpet, or perhaps in the dining room curtains, or a strange formation in the bark of a tree. All these things can be considered illusions, but if we look a little deeper we may discover much more.

I have come across many people in Nottinghamshire who state, often with great pride, that their grandmothers used to read tea leaves. They often go on to say how accurate her predictions were and how they soon came to happen. For those who wish to delve deeper into the mysteries of tea leaf reading, it is necessary to abide by a few ancient guidelines. The cup, and that means cup not mug, must preferably be white or light in colour on the inside. The large-leafed Indian tea, Darjeeling, is said to be the best tea to use, although any tea will do, and for those who do not like tea, coffee grounds may also be read. As the last remaining dregs of tea are poured away, the cup should be turned over and revolved three times while the questioner makes a wish. Finally, it is essential that the reader of the tea leaves is relaxed and in a pleasant frame of mind.

The following list of symbols, which may appear within the cup, are a general guide, and it must be emphasised that there are no hard and fast rules. For those struggling to see images, try squinting your eyes and the symbols may just appear clearer. Should the cup be a mass of leaves, try swilling with a little more tea, and if that does not work remember the saying 'The fuller the cup, the better the luck.'

Aeroplane – Sudden journey, overseas visitor.
Anchor – Success, stability, courage.
Arch – Happy marriage, proposal.
Arrow – Bad news, enemies, loss.
Baby – Pregnancy, ideas, new life chapter.
Ball – Ups and downs, instability.
Balloon – Great future success.
Bat – Enemies, bad news.
Cake – Celebrations, party, anniversary.
Car – Travel, news, visitors, friends.
Cat – Treachery, false friend; however, can mean good luck.
Cross – Troubles, sacrifice, bad news.
Dagger – Jealousy, caution needed.
Dog – Faithful friends, loyalty, admirer.
Dove – Love, contentment, peace.
Egg – Fertility and abundance, wealth, luck.
Envelope – Good news, windfall.
Eye – Watch out, changes on the way.
Feather – Infidelity, instability.
Fire – Do not act in haste.
Fish – Success in everything.
Fork – Major decisions.
Gate – Opportunities, chance in a lifetime.
Glove – A challenge.
Gondola – Romance and travel.
Gun – Violence, danger, enemies.
Hammer – Hard work, success.
Hat – Invitation to a ceremony.
Heart – Love, achievement, harmony.
Horseshoe – Health, wealth, happiness.
House – A move, changes, inheritance.
Initials – Refer to people in the enquirer's life.
Ivy leaf – New friendships, prosperity, good luck.
Jug – Good health, prosperity.

Juggler – New job, new skills, utilitarian abilities.

Key – House move, opportunities, success.

Kite – A wish will be granted.

Knife – A very unlucky symbol.

Ladder – Promotion, achievement.

Loop – Do not be impulsive.

Mermaid – Temptation, infidelity, lies, illusion.

Moon – A love affair.

Moth – Dangerous attractions.

Mushroom – Expansion, sudden change.

Music note – Very good luck.

Nail – Minor illness.

Nurse – Illness on the way.

Oak tree – Strength and success.

Onion – Tears and misfortune.

Owl – Gossip and scandal, false allegations.

Palm tree – Luxury, success, honour, fame.

Pen – Signature required on legal documents.

Pig – Material and spiritual success.

Question mark – Caution will be required.

Rainbow – Future happiness and prosperity.

Rake – New interests, major sort out.

Raven – Illness, visiting a hospital, funeral.

Saw – Interfering relatives and friends.

Scissors – Separation, misunderstanding, an end.

Ship – A foreign admirer, journeys, an emigration.

Spade – Hard work, resulting in major achievement.

Spider – Luck, an admirer who will make themselves known.

Square – Restrictions and hardships.

Star – Wishes will come true.

Table – Invitations, a conference, an interview.

Tower – Entrapment, financial restrictions.

Triangle – Creativity, major new developments.

Umbrella – Protection through a traumatic time.

Unicorn – Achievement of ambitions.

Violin – Romance, entertainment, contentment.

Volcano – Passion and sex, may end in scandal.

Web – A love affair.

Well – Wishes come true.
Wheel – Progress, can mean delays.
Windmill – Adventure and mystery.
Wine glass – Alcoholism, celebrations.
Yacht – Life will suddenly become easier.
Yew tree – Long life.

Witchcraft in Nottinghamshire

There is a common misconception that witches were once burnt at the stake, but this is not entirely true, as execution by this means was usually set aside for traitors and heretics. The average prisoner accused and convicted of witchcraft was publicly executed; a horrible death in which it could take up to 10 minutes for the victim to lose consciousness. The art of hanging with a long drop was not perfected, and the prisoner was basically suffocated or strangled by the rope. When the long drop was introduced, death was almost certainly instantaneous as the spinal column was snapped between the first and second vertebrae.

Witchcraft was not a capital offence in Britain. In 1484 Pope Innocent III declared it a heresy. Between 1066 and 1560 only six people were executed for witchcraft in England: the preference was to exorcise evil spirits and demons from people. During the reign of Elizabeth I the first laws on witchcraft were passed, and in 1604 the statute of James I was introduced: 'An Acte against conjuration Witchcrafte and dealinge with evill and wicked spirits.'

The king was obsessed with witches; he went to trials in Scotland and wrote several books on the subject. James I believed in the Divine Right of Kings, which meant that he considered himself to be God's chosen king upon earth, who would represent God in heaven. This meant that witches, being in league with the Devil, were his worst enemies and must be destroyed at all costs. An estimated 50 people were hanged for practising witchcraft during his reign.

Although torture was illegal, a number of methods were used to identify witches and extract confessions. Searchers would check the victims' bodies for marks of the Devil; any blemish, wart, mole, cut or graze would fit the bill. There was no shortage of evidence, since the majority of the great unwashed were covered with fleas or lice. Another method was to prick the victims with a long needle to see if they bled, and if not it was taken as a sure sign that they were in league with Lucifer. To ensure the right result a 'trick' pricker with a retractable needle, which went up into the wooden handle when pressed against the flesh, was sometimes used, thus causing no pain and leaving no wound. The most infamous method of witch detection was 'ducking'. The accused would have their

Britain was once in the grip of 'Witch Mania'. Thousands of innocent women were persecuted and eventually executed under the accusation of practising the dark arts.

right thumb tied to their left toe and their left thumb tied to their right toe, and then they were thrown into the local pond. If they sank they were innocent, and if they floated they were assumed to be guilty, taken out and executed.

Most of the laws against witchcraft were repealed during the reign of George III. However, suspicion and allegations of liaisons with demons and the Devil continued, particularly in rural villages. In the early part of the 17th century there were a number of entries in the Nottingham Records of women being indicted for witchcraft, and the indictments were transmitted to the Assizes in the following instances:

6 October 1609 – Johanna Clark of Sutton in the Clay, spinster [female spinner] wife of Michael Clark, labourer, 'for witchcraft and for felony'.

12 January 1620–21 – Helen, wife of Bryan Beckett of West Drayton, 'for witchcraft'.

25 April 1623 – the wife of a husbandman at Boughton 'for witchcraft'.

14 July 1623 – Alice, wife of Douglass Busse of Bagthorpe, 'for suspicion of witchcraft'.

The following indictments were dealt with at Sessions:

30 April 1606 – Margaret Frore of Harby, widow, was bound over for her good behaviour for witchcraft.

Witches were thought to cause crops to fail and people to die.

The Kiss of Shame. The Devil was said to initiate witches into his services by making them kiss him.

8 April 1608 – Isabella Cotton of Hayton was charged with 'using charmes' contrary to Statute.

10 July 1609 – Barbara Daste of Broughton Sulney, widow, was charged with being a witch.

2 October 1616 – a warrant was issued against Christian Clark of North Muskham, widow, Elizabeth Hudson of the same place, spinster, and Susan Hodson of the same, spinster, suspected of using incantations against Anna Strey.

15 July 1629 – a warrant was issued against Katherine Brown of Cromwell, widow, for suspicion of witchcraft.

Echoes in Time

Shadow People

Wraiths of Shades

What was that you saw out of the corner of your eye? Did you see it? Was there actually something there? Or, did you imagine it? Maybe you just saw a shadow person.

Paranormal researchers studying this phenomenon say that they are nearly always seen out of the corner of the eye, in the peripheral vision, usually in the dark hours of the morning or very late in the evening. In recent times, more and more people are seeing shadow people straight on and for longer periods. Many state that these shadow people have red glaring eyes, while some are described as having no eyes. Strangely, an increasing number of people are reporting an awareness of eyes but cannot recall exactly what they were like.

Mysterious sightings of shadow people – also known as shadow folk, shadow beings and, in my family, wraiths of shades – have become a hot topic among parapsychologists and ghost-hunters, but what are they and where do they come from? Numerous theories have been put forward.

The Subconscious

Most sceptical people explain shadow people as figments of the imagination or an overtired or stressed mind; strangely, these people seem to have no personal experience of this phenomenon, which, in my book, renders their opinions interesting but not truly helpful. They nearly always go on to say things like 'it was a trick of the light', 'a car headlight cast a shadow in such a way that the imagination perceived it in that way' or 'perhaps you just thought you saw something'. While these explanations can indeed account for some of these phenomena, they can by no means account for the huge percentage of sightings that occur.

The Cloak and Hat Man
This type of shadow person is one of the rarer forms. He appears to follow certain individuals rather then haunt static sites. His eyes glow red and as quickly as he appears he vanishes again.

Ghosts

Typically, shadow people can not be categorised as ghosts as they do not conform to the usual phenomena associated with hauntings and ghostly manifestations. Ghosts, for example, have a distinct human shape with hair, eyes, dateable clothing and a definite countenance. They often appear opaque, cloudy or even only partly there, whereas shadow people have no real shape or definite form; more often than not they are just a dark shape, a silhouette with no clear features. However, they do have a humanoid shape, although details about their appearance are lacking. They also have differing densities of shadow, and some appear very dark while others appear swirling and often misty. One of the main common features of shadow people is their glowing eyes, of contrasting red hues and sizes.

Demons and other Spirit Entities

Many people believe that shadow people are demons or some other nefarious type of spiritual being. This is partly due to the fact that over 70 per cent of people report feeling uneasy or terrified during a sighting or visitation. Their bleak appearance and quick movements, accompanied by an aura of fear, have led some parapsychologists and occultists to believe that shadow people may be some form of demon entity. If they are of demonic origin, perhaps there is a story behind their purpose yet to unfold? It has been suggested that they feed on the vibration of fear. If this is so, then why? Further to this, why do they seem to appear more in certain places or to certain individuals?

Twilight Travellers

Some esoterical schools of thought have suggested that shadow people are not foreign entities or ghosts, but are in fact our own projected souls, travelling astrally out of our bodies, either to the astral planes or the astral world, when we go to sleep at night. This form of the soul projecting itself is called astral travelling or projecting. So what we are actually seeing is not shadow people but a projection of our own souls. This theory seems unlikely considering that most sightings of shadow people are accompanied by a feeling of great unease and dread.

Time Travellers

People from our own future, another idea states, could have found the means to travel to the past – our present. However they are able to accomplish this incredible feat, perhaps in that state they appear to us merely as passing shadows as they observe the events of our timeline.

Interdimensional Entities

Most scientists accept the fact that there are dimensions other than the three that we inhabit. The question is, if these dimensions do actually exist, who or what inhabits them? Some theorists maintain that holdings beyond our own are real and run alongside ours; a few further claim that there could actually be thousands of different dimensions all stacked up against each other like dominoes. If there are inhabitants of these other places, is it possible that they have found a way to interface with our own realities, appearing as dark humanoid shapes to our human eyes? For centuries, psychics and mystics have claimed that there are other dimensions inhabited by otherworldly beings and that we are being visited by them all the time.

Aliens

People who claim to have been abducted by aliens often report that the abducters were 'shadow like', often being able to move through solid walls and doors. Many describe their alien kidnappers as grey in colour and some further state that they are 'hazy'. This has given rise, in some schools of thought, to the idea that shadow people are actually extraterrestrials. The conspiracy theorists maintain that extraterrestrials have a hidden agenda, and their ability to move among humans in a shadowy form makes them less noticeable as they go about their business.

The Mothman

There have been other examples of strange dark figures mysteriously appearing and disappearing again. Some people believe that these dark entities or shadow people are harbingers, portents of doom or a warning that something bad is about to arrive.

The Mothman is a dark, sometimes shadowy figure that allegedly roamed the American state of West Virginia. Among other creatures, he is a topic of interest for cryptozoologists – those who study fabled animals which fall beyond the normal taxonomic classifications.

According to the numerous stories printed, the Mothman was first spotted in November 1966 at a former weapon manufacturing plant in Point Pleasant, West Virginia. Two young people who were on the land said that they had seen a giant, man-sized moth with glowing red eyes, which flew off once it knew it had been spotted. They reported the sighting to local law enforcement, triggering a plethora of

The Whirring Mass
Often appearing as a hazy blur of wispy smoke, this shadow person skulks in the background silently watching.

further sightings, which eased off in December 1967 when the Silver Bridge collapsed, killing 46 people.

Sightings were reported by a wide range of people, typically around dusk or after dark, and some involved paranormal activity such as malfunctioning electronic devices. One report involved a dog that got extremely upset and chased itself round and round; a sign that they are being threatened or attacked from all sides. The next morning, the dog vanished and was never seen again.

Before we go any further with our search into shadow people let us try and categorise exactly what they could be:

Category 1
Mind-altering drugs, epilepsy, drug-induced psychosis and other mental issues. Possible but not likely as hallucinations of a drug-induced origin are usually inconsistent with how shadow people appear. There is a lack of coinciding characteristics and no repeated characteristics from reports of people having used neurotoxic drugs, plants and chemicals. However, there is evidence to suggest that alcohol lowers conscious perceptions to a degree, which makes it more justifiable for shadow people to be seen. Also, tiredness accompanied by small doses of alcohol can have a catalytic value to perception in areas where shadow people are frequently seen or experienced.

Category 2
Ghostly thoughtforms are spirit entities that were once human or of human origin. They are believed to be the result of human emotion – passion, jealousy, anger, pain, love and so on – which, when released from the human body, continue to grow and take form, often appearing at a later date as a full-blown apparition or ghost. This grouping, which is affected by light, falls into the ghost and phantasm category.

Category 3
Maybe shadow people are their own category if we bear in mind that they have several rules which clearly define them. It is quite likely that we do not yet understand the full order of spirits within a universal spiritual hierarchy. Many cultures state that there are orders of spirits in the cosmos, from angels to demons, with numerous other spiritual entities that reside in between, including elementals or lesser evolved spiritual entities (LESE).

Shadow people always appear as shadowy, frequently male, figures and are normally associated with a particular place, often isolated and in a fundamentally lonely rural setting. They are described as having red eyes and are often seen wearing what appears to be a brimmed hat. More often than not they are said to be slim, although small childlike figures have been reported. They can vanish at will and climb walls or ceilings, and there can be as many as 20 seen at one time or as few as one. Shadow people are rarely attracted to anyone in particular, although when they do focus on one person, it is believed that they want or require something from them — what exactly that might be remains elusive. Some researchers believe it is possibly a type of extruded energy, or that they are attempting to communicate with that person, perhaps because the person has an as yet unrealised ability to communicate back.

In my family we do not claim to know exactly what these wraiths of shades are; we just accept that they exist. My family belief system is animistic, meaning that we believe everything — trees, flowers, rocks, water and so on — has a soul, a spirit

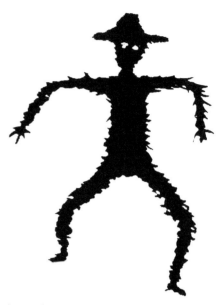

The Spidery Spectre

Perhaps the most common of the three types of shadow people, it is often seen in groups of three or more.

that inhabits it. We believe in a complex order of spirits that exists within our universe. It is impossible to understand everything but, having said that, it is not impossible to respect what we do not understand. As a child I was taught words of summoning to summon these spirits and at the same time the words that dispel them. In my experience, the appearance of shadow people can be a difficult problem to solve or keep at bay, but my family solution to this concerns gathering and using certain herbs, plants, soils and salts, which seem to do the trick. I remember asking my father what the shadows were that crept up the walls after I went to bed at night. He simply looked at me with slight surprise and said 'Get used to it Gossin, [the Irish word for child], for out of the shadows will come shapes, it's just the way it is!' He didn't actually know, but he accepted it as his father had accepted it before him and so forth.

Category 4

Hypnagogic and hypnopompic hallucinations occur when one is in a sleep state (hypnagogic — falling asleep, hypnopompic — waking up). These states are also known as waking-sleep and the visions were once labelled night nurse syndrome, as workers in hospitals, often suffering from overtiredness, would nod off only to find that they were experiencing auditory, visual, sensory and olfactory hallucinations. The person can be conscious and aware of their immediate environment and yet at the same time be in a dream-like state. The phenomenon is well recorded within the scientific field.

Many mediums claim that the trance-like states that they put themselves into are a direct result of achieving a balance between the hypnagogic and hypnopompic states. This 'Third Way,' as it is known, is when the conscious and subconscious mind are in an even balance,. It is then that worlds of the dead can be clearly perceived.

Regardless of any of these theories, shadow people are being seen in ever-increasing numbers. Across Nottinghamshire, and the UK in general, people are telling me of their experiences with these mysterious and often frightening shadow people more and more frequently. The following excerpts are from people who have no axe to grind in relation to the subject matter (some names have been changed to protect identities):

Story One

One night I awoke to find that I could not move. Although I couldn't move my head, I was facing the bedroom door. Standing in the doorway was the dark shape of a man; he just stood there and watched me. I felt terrified, as I lived alone and knew that whoever he was he shouldn't be there. I remember thinking 'Oh God help me', as I thought he was going to do something terrible to me. I then noticed that instead of eyes there were two glowing red eyes that glowed malevolently at me. I knew I had to do something and with every bit of strength I had, I reached out for a glass of water that was on my bedside cabinet and threw it at him. As soon as I did this, the figure just vanished into thin air. I was so terrified afterwards that I had to call my sister at 4am to come over and stay with me.

Janet – Carlton

Story Two

My wife and I moved into a small cottage near Mapperley in 2004. We had a bit of work to do on the building and we made alterations to the layout. Nothing peculiar happened for several months and we lived there quite happily. One night my wife woke me up at 3.10am and said that she had just seen a dark figure pass our bedroom door, and she thought it was a burglar. Terrified, I went to investigate, but searching the house revealed nothing untoward and, after checking all the windows and doors, which showed no signs whatsoever of having been tampered with or opened, I returned to bed and teased my wife about it being a ghost.

Several weeks later, the same thing happened again. At about 3am my wife shook me from sleep and said that once again she had awoken to see the dark silhouette of a man stood in the doorway. He suddenly moved when he noticed her looking at him. I jumped out of bed and went to investigate, once again nothing untoward had happened. The following week the same thing happened again and then again a few nights after that. My wife was becoming increasingly distressed and said she was afraid to sleep at night for fear of what she had now begun to call 'the Dark Man'.

Things took a turn for the worse and the sightings became more and more frequent. In the end I couldn't even joke about it as the very mention of it distressed my wife, who was beginning to look very tired due to lack of sleep and fear, so we decided to move home.

In the early hours of the morning on the day we were moving, I woke up at 3am to find, stood in the doorway, the dark figure of a man. I watched it for several minutes; I was terrified as I knew that what I was looking at was some kind of phantom. I could just make out its eyes, they were glowing a dull red. I felt my wife shake me and whisper 'John, John it's back.' 'I know,' I replied and sitting up in bed with my eyes fixed firmly on it, I watched it move out of sight. Following it, I found the same scenario as always, nothing was there.

John – Southwell

Story Three

When I was a kid we used to live in a big old house near the city centre, I am now 23 and I can still remember very clearly the scary things that used to go on in that house. I must have been about nine years old when I first experienced the dark shadows that used to crawl out of the darkness after I went to bed at night. It really started to happen more after my grandma died; I was very close to her and really missed her after she had gone. I think I had vaguely noticed them before that but after she died it got really bad…There were several of them; the ones I particularly remember were the spidery ones. Thin dark shapes with long skinny arms that crept across the walls and ceiling. I could see them clearly when I squinted my eyes, they moved in a weird way, quickly and with purpose they would skit across the room…On occasion I would wake up and see them staring at me. One of them wore a hat and had red eyes, and if I focused on a particular one it would stand still and vanish. I wouldn't ever go back and stay in that house even if you paid me.

Jenny – Calverton

Story Four

It was years ago when I saw this shadowy ghost. I used to go and stay with my gran in her flat, and I slept on the settee, which was a pull-out bed. I remember waking up and seeing a dark shape of a man in the room, and I would get frightened and run to my gran's room and jump into bed with her. She would just cuddle up and stroke my hair until I went back to sleep. I never told her about the shadowy figure. I remember one night waking up and seeing it stood by the fireplace. The room was dark but it somehow seemed darker, a blackness against the darker shadows, and I knew it was a man. That particular night was really scary as it laughed at me, pointed and then turned into the fireplace and vanished.

Annie – Wollaton

Story Five

I had been married for just six months when I encountered these ghosts. We had just moved into a brand new house, we were its first occupants. The house was built in the grounds of an old manor house. Our bedroom window overlooked an old cottage garden which still had the original water well that supplied water to the house, and actually still worked. The well had a circular stone wall around it, quaint with English cottage garden plants growing around it, just like in a picture postcard. My wife worked as a nurse on nights and one particular night, when she was at work, I woke up in the early hours, you know like when you open your eyes and you are wide awake. The room was brightly lit by the light of the moon and I just thought that's why I had woken up; I am one of those people that can't sleep with a light on, or any other kind of light in the room, I sleep best in the total darkness. I went over to the window to pull the curtains and happened to glance out into the garden. To my surprise I could see several dark figures in the garden, moving around in the moonlight. Intrigued, I stood slightly back from the window in a bid to observe what was happening, hoping I wouldn't be noticed. What I saw amazed me – there, surrounding the old well, must have been six or seven dark figures. Two or three of them were moving about slowly while the others stood very still. As I watched I could see the tallest one move towards the well, he was about seven foot tall with long skinny legs and arms. What happened next still spooks me when I think about it now. Large dark shadows, like hooded figures, started to crawl out of the well. They had no real clear features, just black human shapes with wiry limbs, like spiders. They just crawled out, and it was as if the tall thin shadow was waiting for them. Several of them had glowing eyes and the tall one seemed to have a long face. Completely terrified at this point, I started going around the house and putting all the lights on. I went and put the fluorescent garden lights on, and for the rest of the night I left every light on in the house and garden. Whatever it was that I saw that night, I never want to see it again…it wasn't so much seeing them as much as the feeling of total dread that accompanied the experience.

Jason – West Bridgford

Story Six

It was a dark and stormy night the night it happened! I was 26 years old at the time. I have been seeing shadowy ghost forms all my life. I usually see the coat-and-hat type, but I have never seen them as clearly as I did that night. Perhaps it was the electrical charge in the air, caused by the storm. I lived with parents, and it was late at night. The storm had been rumbling around us for several hours, but as it got to 11.30pm the heavens opened up and torrential rain came down. Mum and Dad had gone to bed, and I decided to watch some television. As I lay there on the settee, feeling kind of uneasy because of the thunder, I noticed a dark figure out of the corner of my eye. It moved towards me really fast, and I could see that it was about 6ft tall with what looked like a long coat. I jumped up with a start, but there was nothing there. I thought it must be the storm making me nervous, so I sat back down and the same thing happened again, so I decided to turn the lights up from the dimmer switch. Returning to the settee, I lay down and watched some more television and it happened again, but by this time I was getting really spooked by it. Morbidly fascinated by it, I lay down again – only this time there wasn't one but four in the room, and I could also see the outline of another stood outside the patio door.

Since that night I have seen the odd one here and there but never as many as the amount I saw on that stormy night…I have got used to them now, and I know that if I stare right at them they just recede into the shadows or run away.

Clair – Mansfield

Story Seven

My daughter first started seeing shadow things (as she calls them) when she was about four years old. She used to get really terrified by them and would come screaming out of her bedroom saying 'nasty man, nasty man is standing behind my door watching me'. On one particular occasion, we were sat at the kitchen table eating dinner. I had my back to the kitchen door, which led to the main house. I kept prompting my daughter to eat her dinner. She was a fussy eater at the best of times, and she just replied 'I can't mummy the shadow thing keeps peeping at me from there', pointing beyond the kitchen towards the living room. I remember feeling a cold shiver run up my spine, and since that day I have never sat with my back to the living room again.

Later that day, after I had dropped my daughter at nursery, I was going from the utility room to the upstairs of the house taking some laundry. As I came back downstairs I walked into the living room and there in front of me was a dark shadowy figure. It vanished as soon as I looked at it, yet it had remained there long enough for me to have had a good look at it. It was very tall and seemed to be wearing some kind of cloak. It was just a dense dark colour, and apart from the gown or cloak it was wearing I couldn't make out any other features.

Tina – Newark

Story Eight

My brother and his friend had an encounter with a shadow ghost in Sherwood Forest. They had gone there camping as teenagers when they were about 18, and you know what teenagers are like, they had taken beer with them and were just kicking back and having fun chatting when the next thing they could hear noises of breaking twigs and leaves being moved. Then out of the bushes dashed this black figure, no more then 10ft away from them. My brother and his friend described it as being about four feet tall and having no shape, just a black mass of shadows. He said it stopped and looked at them before speeding off back into the bushes on the opposite side from where it had come from.

Liz – Nottingham city centre

Story Nine

We used to live in a big Victorian house just on the outskirts of the city centre; the house never had a good feeling to it, it was a gloomy place. Lots of strange things happened in the house that can't be explained. We used to see this black shadow that lurked near the staircase. My two brothers, sister and parents all saw it over a period of about five years. My eldest sister, who didn't live at home, had become a drug addict, so Mum and Dad talked her into coming to live back with them. I guess they figured they could help her. Just after she moved back in, things got really bad. The drugs made her do bad things, and she would steal things and shout and scream when she didn't get her own way.

Everyone started to see even more shadowy ghosts and up to a dozen appearances were made by them in any one day. There wasn't just one anymore either, there were sometimes two or three. They were all very tall, I would say about 7ft, and they moved really fast. One day, when my sister was out, I heard whispering coming from her bedroom. It sounded like two or three male voices, so I bent down and looked through the keyhole, but what I saw shocked me. I could see the dark figure, kind of a silhouette, of a tall man. He had his back to me, and as I looked he turned around and, although he had no obvious face, he stared right at me. Terrified I ran back to my own bedroom, locked the door, immediately logged onto the internet and started reading passages from an online Bible. This didn't help the situation, as my bedroom door began to shake. It was really frightening.

For nearly seven months we continued to see these ghostly black figures, but whenever you looked right at them they seemed to dissolve into thin air or run into the walls. There was always something going wrong with electrical things too. The television would switch itself over, the washing machine would start itself with nothing in it, things blew up and we must have replaced three electric kettles, a toaster and a fridge in those few months.

Eventually my sister kicked her drug addiction, and the haunting of the shadowy ghosts calmed down and eventually stopped. I remain convinced to this day that those creatures were actually some kind of demons made worse by my sister's addiction.

Andy – Trowell

Nottinghamshire Churches and Cathedrals

Southwell Minster

Southwell Minster is truly one of England's most beautiful cathedrals and is a definite jewel in the crown of Nottinghamshire. With its majestic Norman nave and glorious 13th-century chapter house, it has been described as one of England's best-kept secrets.

The Minster church was first established in 965. In 1108 the Normans decided to rebuild it and work was eventually completed by 1150. During the Civil War the structure was seriously damaged by Scottish troops, who completely destroyed the Archbishop's Palace. In 1881 the Minster's distinctive and decorative 'pepperpots' (spires of lead), unique in the United Kingdom, were added to the west towers.

Southwell Minster.

The building is home to several Green Men — carved figures representing the Pagan belief in an ancient fertility god known as Father of the Forest, Jack-in-the-Green or Man of the Wood — that tell us of a significantly different spiritual following prior to Christianity. Many such figures, including Sheela-na-gigs, were incorporated into church buildings, perhaps as a warning not to follow the old ways (or alternatively as a comforter to those that did). This probably made Christianity more palatable to the hardened few who found converting difficult.

The cathedral has very little ghostly activity, although I am told that on certain summer evenings a humming sound can be heard emanating from the building, as if monks are chanting. Also the ghostly figure of a priest is said to walk the building and is seen near to the west wing.

St Mary's Church, Edwinstowe

The impressive 12th-century building of St Mary's Church is said to be the place where Robin Hood married his true love, Maid Marian. Attractions include a beautiful parish tapestry, the carved stone heads of Archbishop Thomas Becket and King Henry II, a mysterious face in the stained-glass east window and a 'Forest Measure' set into the wall to the left of the memorial to the Rigley and Ward families. This is believed to be an ancient rule for measuring land, but it bears no relation to any known unit of measurement, except perhaps a fathom. The building is said to be the haunt of a white nun and a green man, who is said by some to be Robin Hood.

One has only to look closely at the exterior and interior of Nottinghamshire churches to see a wealth of iconic mysteries.

Worksop Priory

For nearly 1,000 years the beautiful church of Worksop Priory has been the home of a Christian community. In 1103 the Great Priory of Our Lady and St Cuthbert at Radford, near Worksop, was founded.

The canons of St Augustine worshipped together in the specified part of the Great Priory Church. Many of the canons were priests, teachers and scholars, so it is no surprise that England's first elementary school was founded here in the 16th century.

Ghosts that haunt the building include a nun, a grey man and a phantom that walks the church interior; its feet may be heard thudding on the iron mesh floor grates. One man is said to have had an encounter with a scented ghost during an Easter vigil inside the church.

Worksop Priory — One of the many jewels in Nottinghamshire's crown, the priory is home to several ghosts, including one that leaves behind a phantom fragrance.

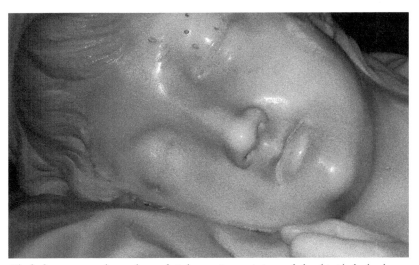

The dead are not at rest here as the sound of phantom footsteps is frequently heard inside the church.

He stayed in the church overnight, as is the custom of the Easter vigil, and in the early hours of the morning he was overwhelmed by the fragrant scent of roses. So strong was the smell that it clung to his clothes. The next morning the priest came to relieve him of his duty, and he recounted the events of his ghostly experience. The vicar just gave him a knowing smile and told him that nothing could harm him in the house of God.

A Haunted Stone

On 7 July 1817 Elizabeth Shepherd, aged 17, left her mother in their comfortable warm home at Papplewick and made her way to Mansfield to seek employment. Elizabeth (Bessie) had reached Harlow Wood when she encountered a Sheffield man, Charles Rotherham. Rotherham, believing that Bessie would have some money on her, set about Bessie with a hedge-stake, violently bludgeoning her to death, and no mercy was shown. On examining her body Rotherham found no money on her person, so he took the girl's shoes and a cotton umbrella that she was carrying.

When Bessie did not return home, her mother made a search and the battered, blood-soaked body of the teenage girl was found. A hue and cry was raised, and Rotherham was arrested 10 days later at the Three Crowns Inn at Redhill, Mansfield, where he had been trying to sell the shoes and umbrella. Charles Rotherham was executed at Gallows Hill on 28 July 1817.

The local community, shocked by the incident, were determined that Bessie should never be forgotten. Mr Anthony Buckles, along with other gentlemen of Mansfield, erected a stone in memory of the tragedy. It remains there today, located in a small hollow, which is said to have an eerie feeling to it, close to the Harlow Wood. The stone reads:

> This stone is erected to the memory of Elizabeth Shepherd, of Papplewick,
> who was murdered while passing this spot by Charles Rotherham,
> July 7th, 1817. Aged 17 years.

Shortly after Bessie's murder, reports began to surface of her ghost being seen on the road. Numerous people claimed to have seen the spirit wandering the verges of the road looking unhappy and lost. Some people feared to travel the road after darkness for fear of meeting her. According to local legend, if the stone that commemorates her death is ever moved then she will rise from her grave and make her presence known. Some years ago a car skidded off the road and collided with the stone. Shortly afterwards a young couple reported seeing a white figure hovering above the stone, which vanished when they approached it. Some local teenagers have been known to visit the stone and circle it three times, then knock on it three times. This is believed to call Bessie from the grave, and she appears in all her blood-stained gore.

Trent Bridge

Who can say, unless have entered into the particular dark mindset, what it is truly like to feel so unhappy, so wracked with emotional stress, isolated and alone, and so desperate to make the torment end that the only way to stop the never-ending pain is to commit suicide?

Over the years numerous people have launched themselves into eternity from the top of Trent Bridge, and stories concerning strange lights and shadowy figures on the bridge are plentiful. Other ghosts seen in the area include a boatman wearing a cloth cap, a cream shirt with braces and smoking a clay pipe as he rows along the river, before vanishing into the murky waters. A blue light has also been reported coming from beneath the dark waters. It moves slowly and purposely up the river, before fading away just as it gets to the Trent Bridge.

Extraterrestrials

Unidentified Flying Objects

The UFO phenomenon consists of thousands of reports of unusual flying objects seen in the skies, which remain unexplained after investigations to ascertain the origins of the objects. UFOs first became popular in the United States in 1947 when a pilot reported seeing nine unusual objects flying over the state of Washington. Since 1947 the US Federal Government, private research institutions, individual scientists and other leading researchers throughout the world have collected data about UFOs. They are by no means unique to the western world, although America and the United Kingdom seem to have taken an active lead in collecting and publishing sighting reports. Other countries such as Mexico, India and China are experiencing an increase in sightings and are developing very good methods of collating and classifying the information.

Most UFO sightings can be explained by atmospheric conditions, normal aircraft activity and hot air balloons, but the quest to establish extraterrestrial visitation has not been made easy by certain individuals who attempt to debunk reports as nonsense or flagrantly imply that anyone who claims to have seen a UFO must be abnormal or suffering from a mental health condition. This is further complicated by groups and individuals who claim to have met with aliens and visited their planets. Some psychics and mystics have claimed to be in contact with otherworldly beings via telepathic or astral means, and further assertions concerning conspiracy theories, world infiltration and domination by an alien species further complicates an already clouded issue.

In the 1960s people started reporting that they were being abducted by aliens, and in America in 1998 the Roper Poll of 5,995 adults suggested that as many as one million Americans believed that they had been abducted. Here in the UK the proportion was considerably lower.

Today the UFO phenomenon is persisting and researchers continue to investigate sightings, although such pursuits are scorned by certain academics and scientists. This is a shame as, presumably, it would be naïve to believe that this world contains the only sentient life forms in the universe. Individuals are becoming less bothered by ridicule, and new and interesting stories are emerging all the time. Unfortunately, most branches of science will never take the subject matter seriously until a real alien, or at the least material of definite extraterrestrial origin, can be produced and examined.

In recent years there have been hundreds of reported sightings of UFOs in Nottinghamshire. On Wednesday 22 May 1991 dozens of people reported seeing a group of UFOs flying in formation across Nottinghamshire. The vast majority of stories corroborate the facts of these reported sightings. On another occasion, over 100 witnesses reported seeing two triangular objects flying in from the east over Calverton, Bestwood and Bulwell. These mysterious objects were last seen moving rapidly over the Ilkeston area in a westward direction. Included in the witness list were a solicitor, nurse, scientist, doctor and a police officer, as well as a miner, road sweeper, barmaid and bricklayer.

The following is a selection of stories related to me by some of the people of Nottinghamshire, and I must stress at this point that those whose stories I have included strike me as balanced individuals who have nothing to gain by inventing, elaborating or embroidering what they fundamentally believe they have seen or experienced.

Strange unidentified flying objects seen over the skies of Nottinghamshire are frequently reported. Many sightings still go unexplained and there is increasing evidence that we are not alone.

Story One – November 2000

I was staying with my grandmother; we were sitting in the garden on a warm summer night in June, just whiling away the time chatting about anything and everything. Gran had just gone to get us another drink when I noticed a series of three bright lights shining in the sky. The sun was just setting, and my original thoughts were that it was evening stars, but then I knew this couldn't be right as I was used to seeing sunsets and I knew that no stars made that type of formation.

Gran came back and I pointed the three bright lights out to her, we were both fascinated and watched the objects for another minute or so before one of them broke away and made a zigzag pattern across the sky, we both sat there fascinated by what we were witnessing. Suddenly they shot off at great speed, it was as if they knew we were looking at them and vanished because of it.

April – Hucknall

Story Two – January 1996

I live in the Eastwood area and my neighbour, who is elderly, telephoned me at around 10.30am to say there were lights hovering in the sky just outside her bungalow, these lights were making her feel uneasy. My son and his girlfriend agreed to go over there and investigate what was happening, I was happy for them to go as I was busy cooking the dinner. Later my son returned home and told me that there were indeed lights in the sky that glowed red and then orange and moved in a peculiar way. As time went by, they eventually vanished and reappeared one at a time in a distinct formation, apparently they were moving in a slow and definite pattern and every now and again would stop and wait for some of the others to catch up. My son took photographs with his mobile phone, they appeared spherical, and my son and his girlfriend maintain that they made no obvious noise whatsoever.

The strange lights stayed there for some time, at one point my son and his girlfriend said that the lights were accompanied by five or six smaller blue lights. Then a larger silver-coloured light joined the formation, and about 30 seconds later the larger silver object abruptly shot off in an easterly direction and the others followed. These lights, which I truly believe were UFOs, must have been seen by other people.

Shirley – Eastwood

Story Three – 29 October 2000

I was out walking my dog in the late afternoon when I noticed a strange cigar-shaped aircraft hovering in the sky just above an outcrop of trees. It must have been at least 40ft long based on the size of the trees it was hovering over. Standing there staring at the object gave me a very peculiar feeling, it all just seemed so surreal. My dog never even barked, he showed no reaction to the object whatsoever. I would describe the aircraft as being a silvery blue colour with what appeared to be holes along its side, possibly lights or windows. It stayed there for another five minutes and I just watched it, then it started to move in an upward direction at an incredible speed; it stopped again for about 10 or 20 seconds before moving off at a steady speed, I would estimate it to be moving about 50 miles an hour. Amazed at what I had just seen, I made my way home.

Over the next few days I kept an eye on the newspapers and listened to the news, but there was no mention of the strange airship.

Jon – Beeston

Story Four – July 2006

In July 2006 I witnessed some really unusual lights that flew over my house travelling north to south in a triangular formation. There were two orange lights and the lead one was bright silver, they couldn't have been part of the same object as they were too far apart from each other.

It had been a warm few weeks and the weather had been really nice. I was sat in the garden having a refreshing drink after a long warm day. The sky was cloudless and I could see that some of the stars were out already; as I sat there I noticed two or three aircraft pass over with their usual flashing lights, towards East Midlands Airport, and I could even hear the faint hum of their engines.

Suddenly streaming across the sky was a bright white ball of light. At first I thought it was a shooting star but it maintained a direct path, was lower than the aircraft I had not long witnessed and had no flashing lights. As quickly as it appeared, it moved across the sky and vanished out of sight. I just thought it was odd but didn't give it another thought, and I went to get myself another drink. Shortly after I had come back out into the garden the light reappeared, only this time it was accompanied by two orange lights and, unlike last time, they moved across the sky in an east to west direction but much slower. I watched them for two or three minutes, and they seemed much larger than an aircraft. They made no noise and their movement was steady with purpose.

Chris – Ravenshead

Creswell Crags

Creswell Crags – a Site of Special Scientific Interest – lies on the border of Nottinghamshire and Derbyshire. It is a limestone gorge honeycombed with caves and smaller fissures. Being one of the most northerly places on earth to have been visited by our ancient ancestors, a fact which is unique on a world scale, Creswell Crags is a fascinating historical time capsule. Archaeological remains of animals and stone tools have been found in the caves, which appear to have been used by Ice Age hunters who came to track and hunt the herds of mammoth, reindeer and bison as they migrated to their spring and summer grazing pastures.

The caves are unique, and archaeologists have found the earliest known examples of prehistoric cave art, carved by ancient Britons, in Church Hole Cave, which dates back 12,000 years. The discovery in 2003 triggered a major buzz among scientists and archaeologists, as it fills a major gap in the country's archaeological record. Before the find at Creswell Crags, the best-known examples of such art were found at Altamira in Spain, and Lascaux and Chauvet in France. Scientists are also hailing Creswell Crags as the 'oldest habitation in Britain!'

The sequence of human occupation at Creswell is thought to have begun around 45,000 years ago with the Neanderthals. They lived in many of the caves, which have been given

Creswell Crags. The caves at Creswell Crags are unique and archaeologists have found the earliest known examples of prehistoric cave art, carved by ancient Britons, in Church Hole Cave, which dates back 12,000 years. A hideous old hag haunts the vicinity as well as a Roman soldier.

fanciful names following 19th-century archaeological discoveries, such as Church Hole, Mother Grundy's Parlour, Pin Hole and Robin Hood's Cave (the largest of the caves). The discoveries at Creswell include a fish pattern on a mammoth's tusk, the figure of a masked man carved on a section of bison bone, a reindeer rib adorned with a chevron pattern and, oldest of all, the figure of a horse's head carved on another piece of rib bone. Utensils and weapons have also been found, including a spectacular dagger created from the spine of a mammoth and drinking vessels produced from rhinoceros bones.

Ghosts have been reported at Creswell Crags for many years now and the most eminent of them is a witch who has been seen on numerous occasions at differing places on the site. During the 1980s a couple were on their way home after a day out when they halted at a set of temporary traffic lights near to the visitor centre at Creswell Crags. Despite the day being unusually warm, the couple felt a cold chill and the lady happened to glance through the window, but what she saw terrified her. There, in a tangle of brambles, weeds and undergrowth she could see a strange pinkish blur of what, at first, she thought was a basketball. It appeared to be hovering several feet off the ground, and straining her eyes to see what it was, she was shocked to find that it resembled the withered face of a woman. Before she had a chance to react, the shape began to float backwards and forwards as if it were being manipulated via invisible strings like a puppet. As she watched, horrified yet fascinated, the face began to visibly change, becoming much clearer. She later described the figure as 'an old hag' with grotesquely dark eyes and a beaked nose. Thinking that it must be a practical joke, and that somebody must be hiding in the bushes and working a puppet, she tried to consciously view the unusual happening with sceptical logic. However, the longer she watched the strange shape, the clearer it became; it seemed to shift and change until, finally, it resembled a woman with a pale and haggard face. Warts and skin blemishes could clearly be seen, and her eyes had a cold glint of malice and appeared to 'pierce the soul'. The figure began to move towards the car, at which point the women screamed and her husband, shocked at what was now happening, sped off.

When the shocked woman reached home, a doctor had to be called who prescribed a sedative to calm her down. The doctor believed it was a prankster who needed to be stopped in case they caused an accident, so he telephoned the police. They searched the area, but there appeared to be nothing untoward. One of the policemen went into the thicket to see if he could see any signs of a trick having been played on the couple. He was badly scratched in the process, ripped his uniform and received further cuts from the brambles. Later he declared that it would have been impossible, due to the density of the undergrowth, for anyone to have hidden in there to play a trick of that sort.

Later that night there was another report by a truck driver who claimed that he was forced to brake abruptly near the same spot, when he encountered a mysterious dark figure dashing out in front of him before vanishing into thick bushes. Shaken by his encounter, he described the figure as headless, but mentioned that it seemed to float across the road. Although he could not see its face, he knew that it was female.

Other spirits at Creswell include a headless phantom seen in Robin Hood's Cave, a Cavalier in full regalia seen brandishing a sword, strange globular lights of differing colours, shades seen in several areas in and around the site, and a snarling beast heard in the vicinity of Pin Hole Cave.

Cryptozoology

The word cryptozoology comes from the Greek kryptos meaning hidden, zoo meaning animal – those which exist outside of the modern zoological categories – and logos meaning knowledge; literally, the study of hidden animals. Cryptozoology basically consists of two areas of research; firstly, the search for animals that can be identified through fossil records, living dinosaurs or animals believed to be extinct; and secondly, creatures of folklore, legend and myth that are periodically claimed to be seen by individuals or groups of people. Those that study the subject are known as cryptozoologists, while the animals that they study are referred to as cryptids, a term coined by John Wall in 1983. Cryptozoology is considered a pseudoscience because of the lack of scientific method.

Mysterious large black cats are disturbingly being seen with ever-increasing regularity. So far they have been spotted in Sherwood Forest, Newark, Mansfield and Kirkby in Ashfield, usually in a wooded or rural location.

The Unicorn.

The Mermaid.

The Griffin.

The Phoenix.

Examples of cryptids include Bigfoot, the Loch Ness Monster and the Beast of Bodmin. Worldwide, there are dozens of others. The vast majority of cryptid sightings are usually hoaxes, misinterpretations of natural phenomena or misidentification. The internet is home to thousands of websites dedicated to the subject, and there an increasing number of people are becoming interested in it. Also on the increase are claims of sightings of weird, wonderful and exotic arrays of fabled animals. Despite this, cryptozoology has a greater amount of failures then successes. One would think in this digital age, with mobile camera phones and market demand reducing the price of cameras and video equipment, that more and more people would be capturing these mysterious creatures on film, but alas this is not happening. However, there are ever-increasing reports of strange creatures being seen in the woods and countryside of Nottinghamshire. In Sherwood Forest, there have been numerous sightings of a large ape-like creature, and there is even video footage of the supposed creature.

By far the most common sightings in Nottinghamshire, and indeed the Midlands, are large black cats. These mysterious creatures are being seen regularly, and so far they have been spotted in Sherwood Forest, Newark, Mansfield and Kirkby in Ashfield, usually in a wooded or rural location. Some researchers claim that the big black cats, sometimes dogs, are in fact alien visitors in the guise of these animals; why an alien would believe that they would go unnoticed in the English countryside in such a disguise is beyond me. Other reports state that they may well be panthers that have escaped from private animal collections or zoos.

Other strange creatures include a large black slug-like being, a huge black bird and a giant snake seen near Carlton. Whatever these creatures are – be they of supernatural, natural or imaginative origins – they will continue to fascinate and frighten people for some time to come. Meanwhile the search for cryptids will go on and interest in cryptozoology will continue to grow.

Newstead Abbey

Newstead Abbey is perhaps better known for one of its previous owners – the poet, Lord Byron. The original building was an Augustinian priory founded by Henry II in about 1170. A small religious community existed on the site until Henry VIII dissolved the monasteries in 1539. The following year Henry VIII granted Newstead to one of Lord Byron's ancestors, Sir John Byron, who set about converting the priory into a house for the use of his family. Today the monastic chapter house has survived and has been used as a chapel since the time of the Byrons.

Newstead remained in the Byron family until the poet sold it to Thomas Wildman in 1818. Wildman had inherited a vast fortune from plantations owned by his family in Jamaica. He spent this wealth restoring and repairing Newstead, which was in a dilapidated state when he purchased it. He employed the architect John Shaw to carry out alterations yet keep the medieval theme; most importantly, he was to blend any new alterations into the existing character of the house. Ancient armour, tapestries and elaborate antique furniture was purchased to furnish the house, thus staying with the theme.

In 1861 William Frederick Webb, friend of Dr David Livingstone, purchased the abbey from the widow of Thomas Wildman. The chapel was redecorated, but the rest of the house has remained largely unchanged. When Mr Webb passed away in 1899, the estate was passed

Newstead Abbey. The original building was an Augustinian priory founded by Henry II in about 1170. A small religious community existed on the site until Henry VIII dissolved the monastery in 1539.

Near this Spot
are deposited the Remains of one
who possessed Beauty without Vanity,
Strength without Insolence,
Courage without Ferosity,
and all the virtues of Man without his Vices.
This praise, which would be unmeaning Flattery
if inscribed over human Ashes,
is but a just tribute to the Memory of
B.OATSWAIN, a DOG,
who was born in *Newfoundland* May 1803
and died at *Newstead* Nov.r 18th 1808.

When some proud Son of Man returns to Earth,
Unknown to Glory but upheld by Birth,
The sculptor's art exausts the pomp of woe,
And storied urns record who rests below:
When all is done, upon the Tomb is seen
Not what he was, but what he should have been.
But the poor Dog, in life the firmest friend,
The first to welcome, foremost to defend,
Whose honest heart is still his Masters own,
Who labours, fights, lives, breathes for him alone,
Unhonour'd falls, unnotic'd all his worth,
Deny'd in heaven the Soul he held on earth:
While man, vain insect! hopes to be forgiven,
And claims himself a sole exclusive heaven,
Oh man! thou feeble tenant of an hour,
Debas'd by slavery, or corrupt by power,
Who knows thee well, must quit thee with disgust,
Degraded mass of animated dust!
Thy love is lust, thy friendship all a cheat,
Thy tongue hypocrisy, thy heart deceit,
By nature vile, ennobled but by name,
Each kindred brute might bid thee blush for shame.
Ye! who behold perchance this simple urn,
Pass on, it honours none you wish to mourn,
To mark a friend's remains these stones arise,
I never knew but one - and here he lies.

Newstead Abbey. Boatswain's epitaph.

to each of his surviving children, and finally the house came into possession of Charles Ian Fraser, his grandson. Mr Fraser then later sold Newstead to the philanthropist Sir Julien Cahn, who proudly presented it to the Nottingham Corporation in 1931.

A fan of Byron's poetry, Sophie Hyatt, came to live at a farm near to the abbey in the time of Thomas Wildman's occupancy of the house. Sophie was a very shy girl. Being deaf, she did not verbally communicate, and she would always carry a slate tablet on which she would write instructions and any correspondence when necessary. When Thomas Wildman and his wife learned how fond Sophie was of

The poet Byron is said to have encountered numerous ghosts whilst staying at the abbey, he included several of the ghosts in some of his poetical works.

Byron's work, they allowed her to walk in the grounds whenever she wanted, and she would on occasion take one of Byron's dogs for a walk. People would see Sophie out and about walking, often with the dog, and because she was fond of wearing light-coloured clothing she became known as 'Little White Lady of Newstead.'

Sophie was provided for by an income from a relative. In 1825 the relative passed away leaving Sophie without means to survive. Desperate, Sophie decided to travel to America to ask another relative for help. Setting off for Nottingham and planning to take a stagecoach to London and then travel to America, Sophie left the Wildmans a note stating her intent and saying her goodbyes. When Mrs Wildman read the note Sophie

The rooks at Newstead are said to be the departed souls of the Black Friars of the Abbey. They have been seen to observe the Sabbath by not flying out of the grounds.

had already left. She immediately spoke to her husband, and together they dispatched a messenger to find Sophie and offer her permanent accommodation in the grounds of Newstead. The messenger immediately set off in hot pursuit and, reaching the Market Square at Nottingham, he found a crowd gathered next to a horse and cart outside the Black Boy pub. Intrigued, the messenger pushed through the people to find Sophie lying on the cobbles – dead. Not hearing the drayman's warning, she had been run over by a horse and cart. She can now be seen

Boatswains Tomb. The ghost of Byron's dog Boatswain is said to haunt the area immediately near to this elaborate monument.

wandering through the gardens of Newstead, especially along one particular pathway known as White Lady's Walk.

The rooks of Newstead, according to local legend, are said to be the reincarnation of the 'black monks' that once lived there. These rooks were seen to observe the Sabbath and would not fly out of the grounds on a Sunday, although every other day of the week they would fly off to the surrounding countryside to look for sustenance. So strongly was this believed by the local people that the rooks were never shot or harmed in any way. Some people even state that there is a legend similar to that of the ravens at the Tower of London – should these birds ever leave their nesting place then disaster and ruination will soon follow.

During the occupancy of the Byrons, the phantom Black Goblin Friar would appear to the head of the household prior to an unhappy event. This portent is also said to have appeared to the poet Lord Byron shortly before his disastrous marriage to Annabella Milbanke, which lasted for one year. Byron's encounter with the apparition is recalled in his poem *Don Juan (Canto XVI)*:

> As Juan mused on mutability,
> Or on his mistress – terms synonymous –
> No sound except the echo of his sigh

Or step ran sadly through that antique house;
When suddenly he heard, or thought so, nigh,
A supernatural agent – or a mouse,
Whose little nibbling rustle will embarrass
Most people as it plays along the arras.
It was no mouse, but lo! a monk, array'd
In cowl and beads and dusky garb, appear'd,
Now in the moonlight, and now lapsed in shade,
With steps that trod as heavy, yet unheard;
His garments only a slight murmur made;
He moved as shadowy as the sisters weird,
But slowly; and as he pass'd Juan by,
Glanced, without pausing, on him a bright eye.

Juan was petrified; he had heard a hint
Of such a spirit in these halls of old,
But thought, like most men, there was nothing in 't
Beyond the rumour which such spots unfold,
Coin'd from surviving superstition's mint,
Which passes ghosts in currency like gold,
But rarely seen, like gold compared with paper.
And did he see this? or was it a vapour?

Once, twice, thrice pass'd, repass'd – the thing of air,
Or earth beneath, or heaven, or t' other place;
And Juan gazed upon it with a stare,
Yet could not speak or move; but, on its base
As stands a statue, stood: he felt his hair
Twine like a knot of snakes around his face;
He tax'd his tongue for words, which were not granted,
To ask the reverend person what he wanted.

The third time, after a still longer pause,
The shadow pass'd away – but where? the hall
Was long, and thus far there was no great cause
To think his vanishing unnatural:
Doors there were many, through which, by the laws
Of physics, bodies whether short or tall
Might come or go; but Juan could not state
Through which the spectre seem'd to evaporate.

Byron, 1823

Byron also encountered a dark entity in his bedroom, which was located on the west façade of the priory church, known as the Rook Cell. The entity awoke Byron by jumping up and down on his bed; he described it as a black mass with two glowing red eyes (see Shadow People). The phantom then tumbled off the bed and vanished.

A gardener digging in the gardens came across a perfectly-preserved skull, which Byron believed belonged to one of the Black Friars that previously lived at the abbey. The skull was of a large size, and Byron sent it to London to be cut, polished and mounted as a drinking chalice. On its return to Newstead, Byron wrote these words:

> Start not – nor deem my spirit fled
> In me behold the only skull,
> From which unlike a living head,
> Whatever flows is never dull.
>
> I lived, I loved, I quaffed like thee
> I died; let earth my bones resign
> Fill up – thou canst not injure me;
> The worm has fouler lips than thine.
>
> Better to hold the sparkling grape,
> Than nurse the earth – worm's slimy brood
> And circle in the goblet's shape
> The drink of Gods, than reptile's food.
>
> Where once my wit, perchance, hath shone,
> In aid of others let me shine;
> And when, alas! our brains are gone,
> What nobler substitute than wine?'
> 'Quaff while thou canst: another race,
> When thou and thine, like me are sped
> May rescue thee from earth's embrace,
> And rhyme and revel with the dead.'
>
> Why not? Since through life's little day
> Our heads such sad effects produce;
> Redeem'd from worms and wasting clay,
> This chance is theirs, to be of use.

Other ghosts to haunt Newstead include a phantom dog believed to be Byron's Newfoundland dog, Boatswain, which died of rabies in 1808. Byron is said to have stayed by the animal's side day and night, nursing it even when the dog was delirious and dangerously rabid.

The ghost of the dog is seen wandering in the grounds, phantom barks have been heard in the main building and on dark nights the luminous glowing figure of a dog is seen walking in the areas which were once glorious gardens. A former security guard at the abbey came face to face with a snarling white dog one winter's night. He claims that the dog launched itself at him with snarling teeth and saliva pouring from its mouth. Fearing that the dog was going to bite his face, he raised his arms up over his head and waited for the attack, but nothing happened. Lowering his arms and looking around him, he could see no sign of the mysterious animal which had leapt to attack him moments before.

There is a poem engraved on Boatswain's tomb which, strangely, happens to be longer than Byron's. The opening lines, long thought to have been written by Byron, have been found to have been written by his friend John Hobhouse. Byron had originally planned to use just the last two lines as the inscription.

Near this Spot
are deposited the Remains of one
who possessed Beauty without Vanity,
Strength without Insolence,
Courage without Ferosity,
and all the virtues of Man without his Vices.
This praise, which would be unmeaning Flattery
if inscribed over human Ashes,
is but a just tribute to the Memory of
BOATSWAIN, a DOG,
who was born in Newfoundland May 1803
and died at Newstead Nov. 18, 1808.
When some proud Son of Man returns to Earth,
Unknown by Glory, but upheld by Birth,
The sculptor's art exhausts the pomp of woe,
And storied urns record who rests below.
When all is done, upon the Tomb is seen,
Not what he was, but what he should have been.
But the poor Dog, in life the firmest friend,
The first to welcome, foremost to defend,

Whose honest heart is still his Master's own,
Who labours, fights, lives, breathes for him alone,
Unhonored falls, unnoticed all his worth,
Denied in heaven the Soul he held on earth —
While man, vain insect! hopes to be forgiven,
And claims himself a sole exclusive heaven.
Oh man! thou feeble tenant of an hour,
Debased by slavery, or corrupt by power —
Who knows thee well must quit thee with disgust,
Degraded mass of animated dust!
Thy love is lust, thy friendship all a cheat,
Thy tongue hypocrisy, thy words deceit!
By nature vile, ennoble but by name,
Each kindred brute might bid thee blush for shame.
Ye, who perchance behold this simple urn,
Pass on — it honours none you wish to mourn.
To mark a friend's remains these stones arise;
I never knew but one — and here he lies.

Among some of the other frequently ghostly visitors are Little Sir John Byron, who lived at the house in the 17th century and was known as 'Little Sir John with the Great Beard.' By a strange coincidence, Little Sir John passed away on the very same day as his beloved wife, just a few hours apart. Shortly after his death, servants reported seeing his ghost sitting in the library smoking a pipe and reading a book. He is still seen and his pipe tobacco is still smelt today.

The Cavalier Ghost also makes an appearance every so often. He is seen appearing as a light smoke. Byron, the poet, is said to have seen the wispy formations of this ghost emanating out of the floor in his bedchamber. Custodians at the house have reported seeing the Cavalier reflected in a mirror, but when they look towards the area of the room where he should be, there is nothing to be seen except the occasional haze of smoke. The Rose Lady is another ghostly visitor, as is a man in a blue tunic. These ghosts are seen periodically in different parts of the building. Distant visitors to the hall, as well as locals, have many strange and curious tales to tell about their visits:

Story One

Both my mother and I have experienced the Rose Lady. We went on a ghost walk at Newstead Abbey, and as we came to the bottom of a large staircase we could smell the distinct scent of roses. At the time we laughed because we thought it was the guides putting on some effects to make our ghost tour more interesting. At the end of the tour we thanked our tour guide for a very interesting evening. It was at this point that my mother enquired about the rose perfume. She explained to the guide that the smell had taken her back to her childhood and being in her grandfather's garden. The smell was akin to a rose garden after a rainstorm, and she asked to purchase the scent as a room freshener for her own home. The guide looked at her blankly and said 'But madam, we didn't use any perfumes'. Thinking it was part of the script, my mother reiterated her request for the scent, but again the custodian explained that it was not part of the tour and it had never been a theatrical trick. Mother, realising that what we had experienced was probably a ghost, went quite pale; we drove home in complete silence.

Janet – Farndon

Story Two

A few years ago me and my girlfriend went out for a drive. It was a lovely summer evening and we just drove around chatting and taking in the scenery. As it got dark we came near to Newstead Abbey and decided to park up. We sat in the twilight kissing and cuddling, when my girlfriend suddenly said that she could see someone dressed in white moving around in front of the car. I immediately switched on the headlights, but there was nothing visible. Switching the lights back off again, we could both see what appeared to be a white-cloaked figure about 30ft away from the car. It seemed to be hovering, as you could see the ground about 2ft below it, but no legs were apparent.

Michael – Watnall

Story Three

We used to go into the grounds of the abbey when I was a kid in the 1960s. We would get up to the usual mischief that teenagers do. One summer evening we cycled to the abbey from Kirkby in Ashfield, and we intended on lighting a campfire to sit around, chat and have a laugh. There were six of us, all lads, and we had brought food with us as well as some beer. We also planned to try and catch some fish in the nearby lake; if we were very lucky, some big enough to cook and eat.

I was in charge of getting the fire started, while three mates went off to forage for wood and the other two decided to start fishing with makeshift rods cut from a willow tree. As I attempted to kindle the fire, I noticed a black-robed figure stood at the edge of some trees about 500 yards away. I ignored it and thought it was one of the lads trying to spook me; he had probably found a dirty blanket and had wrapped it around himself pretending to be ghostly monk.

I briefly looked down and then looked up again. This time I could clearly see – no more then 30ft away from me – the same figure, only it wasn't a mate playing tricks, as I could clearly see that it was someone in a monk's habit and cowl. I was terrified, and I could make out that the figure had greyish skin and hollow eyes with a very thin face. Needless to say, I took to my heels and started running. Getting my bike, I cycled home as fast as I could. I knew that whatever that thing was, it was evil and it definitely wasn't human; there was no way it could have covered those 500 yards in the time I looked down and up again. When I eventually saw my friends a few days later, they just asked where I had gone, and I told them that I felt ill so came home. Tom said 'Well thanks for lighting the fire before you went.' I could tell they were serious, and I knew that I hadn't lit the fire, so who had?

Jack – Kirkby in Ashfield

Angels and Demons

There was a time when people across Nottinghamshire believed in malevolent spirits (demons) that attempted to sabotage ordinary God-fearing people's daily lives. Today I am increasingly hearing people refer to unpleasant ghostly experiences as demonic. I am

His Satanic Majesty, Lucifer. Instructs his demonic armies to inflict pain and confusion on mankind, his main intention is to make man stray away from God's heavenly intent.

asked all the time to define exactly what an evil spirit is. It is a question that I find hard to answer given the fact that one individual's interpretation of evil doesn't necessarily mean that what they experienced was evil – man inevitably attempts to make sense out of what he experiences and when he can't make sense out of it he immediately places it in a supernatural category, usually with a negative connotation.

So what are demons? It might be easier to approach the concept from a Christian concept. According to Judaic Christian belief, the universe is populated with all sorts of demons and angels, which were in residence long before man was created. Who created all these characters is one of life's little mysteries, but let's go with the theory that there was a great battle and Lucifer was cast down into a fiery pit with all his would-be followers. After all, God presumably didn't create his own enemies, as it wouldn't make any sense, even to those who believe God created everything. These demons were given free reign to wander over the earth creating havoc for mankind. Each demon was given a specific duty, as was each angel in heaven. The angels specifically attempted to counteract the demons. The following is the order of angels and demons:

God

Angels

First Hierarchy
Seraphim
Cherubim
Thrones

Second Hierarchy
Dominions
Principalities
Powers

Third Hierarchy
Virtues
Archangels
Angels

The Devil – Lucifer

First Hierarchy
Asmodeus – avarice
Astaroth – laziness
Balberith – murder
Beelzebub – pride
Gressil – disease
Leviathan – blasphemy
Sonneillon – hatred
Verrine – impatience

Second Hierarchy
Carnivean – obscenity
Carreau – cruelty
Oeillet – greed
Rosier – lasciviousness
Verrier – disobedience

Third Hierarchy
Belais – arrogance
Iuvart – sins not covered by other devils
Olivier – parsimony

The list has been added to over the course of history. In 1608 Friar Francesco Mario Buazzo came up with some demons who worked as servants to the devils:

Fire Demons – live in the air and dominate the other devils.
Aerial Demons – hover around human beings.
Terrestrial Demons – terrorize the inhabitants of forests and fields.
Aqueous Demons – live in water.
Subterranean Demons – live in caves like trolls.
Heliophobic Demons – only emerge at night.

Witches were accused of being in direct contact with demons, beguiling them to do mischief and malice against mankind. Today there is a resurgence of interest in angelic and demonic entities, and more and more often they are creeping into ghost stories and paranormal experiences. One of the most common mentions I hear concerning demons is that of the 'night demon' or the 'sleep terror' that people across Nottingham are reporting with ever-increasing frequency. The 'mare' in nightmare is not a female horse but a 'mara' – an Anglo-Saxon and Old Norse term for a demon that sat on sleepers' chests, causing them to have bad dreams. According to folklore, they can get into your home though windows and doors even if they are shut tight and firmly locked. In the dead of the night, one can hear them scratching in the wall cavities and loft space as they attempt to get in. Night demons come to feed on your life force, the very energy of your soul, and they seek out certain individuals to feed upon.

In the past, iron was hung above beds to keep the night demons at bay, but this didn't always work. People who experience night demons complain of being woken up in the hours of the dead (between midnight and 5am), with what feels like a heavy weight or someone sitting on their chest. They are unable to breathe, and this usually lasts for no more than a few seconds. Many people claim that they can hear the night demon sucking the life from

Angels and Demons. Angels are said to be around us all the time. They intervene with the affairs of men when they are called upon to do so.

Angelology, the study of angels, is becoming a popular subject. There is an increase in angelic intervention being reported all over Nottinghamshire.

their bodies and the air from their lungs; others maintain that night demons are accompanied by a terrible smell or a gushing sound 'like being in a cave behind a waterfall'. Night demons are also believed to follow and feed on old blood (a term meaning old established families), while some mystics claim that they feed from the lifeforce of very spiritual people. Victims of night demons feel exhausted and generally lack concentration for the rest of the day after an attack. According to folklore, there are several ways to stop a night demon from getting access to you:

— Turn your shoes around at the side of the bed, so that the toes point away from you.

— When a night demon is apparent, simply put your thumb in your hand, and he will have to retreat.

— Night demons can also be repelled with horse hair.

— Shout out to the night demon: 'Come tomorrow and drink and eat with me,' and if it has been sent by a witch or enemy then that person will be forced by their own evil eye to call at your house the next day; when they visit, offer them salt and bread to eat.

Charm against Night-Mares – Germany
I lay me here to sleep;
No night-mare shall plague me,
Until they swim all the waters

That flow upon the earth,
And count all the stars
That appear in the firmament!
Thus help me God, Father, Son, and Holy
Ghost. Amen!

The only real known antidote to night demons is holy stones, or hag stones, as they are sometimes called, which have a hole in them that has naturally been eroded by the elements – wind, rain, water, heat and frost – and are often found on beaches or in quarries. These stones not only give absolute protection against night demons, but they also grant the owner visions of events that are yet to come if they hold the stone up to the full moon and peer through the natural piercing.

Duke of Wellington
Kirkby in Ashfield

Believed to be the oldest public house in Kirkby in Ashfield, this lovely inn is home to some very peculiar goings-on. Occupants with dogs have reported that they take to howling and barking in the early hours of the morning and usually in the same place.

The bar is situated in the oldest part of the building, and the ghosts at work here like to stack bar furniture on top of tables. A previous owner reported that every morning, on entering the bar, they would find that all the chairs had been piled on top of the tables, as if they had been stacked ready for the bar to be cleaned. On other occasions they discovered tables and chairs turned over and the whole bar in disarray 'like a bomb had hit it'.

These strange happenings are thought to be connected to some tunnels which are believed to run beneath the pub to the nearby churchyard. A previous worker at the pub reported hearing strange dragging noises coming from deep within the earth. The strange manifestation of a man in a flat cap and herringbone jacket has also been reported. The figure is believed to be a previous customer, who liked the atmosphere of the pub so much that he comes back from the grave now and again for a phantom pint of his old favourite.

The Hemlock Stone

What eyes innumerable, O ancient stone,
Have gazed and gazed thy antique form upon?

The above was written by H.S. Sutton, with reference to the mysterious sandstone outcrop at Bramcote near Nottingham. Nowadays it is popularly known as the Hemlock Stone and goes mostly unnoticed, so much so that it has been removed from the list of Sites of Special Scientific Interest, but the current lack of interest in the stone is a recent development. The legends and folklore embroidered in the history of such stones are an important part of our anthropological folklore and history and we need to stay interested in such things, as to lose or forget these items of antiquity is surely to lose and abandon ourselves.

According to local legend, the Hemlock Stone was thought to have been hurled at Lenton Priory, nearly four miles west of the stone, by his Satanic Majesty himself. Reference to the Devil or some other diabolical monster hurling rocks at religious or sacred places is commonplace in British folklore and emphasises the tension that was felt between Christians and Pagans in the past.

The Hemlock Stone was apparently thrown from a hill above Castleton in Derbyshire. Standing on this hill is Peveril Castle and below it is the Treak Cliff Cavern, the home of the famous Blue John gemstone. This massive limestone cave is said to be one of several supernatural entrances to the 'Underworld' in England and is the home of goblins and sprites. When heavy rain falls from the cavern, the locals say it is the Devil urinating!

In the past, the Hemlock Stone was venerated as a sacred place. On the ancient Pagan festival of Beltane (1 May), a fire was lit on top of the stone in a bid to guide the good spirits back to earth to help the living with their daily lives. Beltane, meaning bright fire, was a celebration of life and the return of summer to the world. Fires were often lit at sacred places and standing stones in celebration of a prosperous and fertile year ahead.

Close to the Hemlock Stone there once existed the 'Sick Dyke,' a natural water spring that was thought to have miraculous healing powers. The waters were especially good for treating

In times past the Hemlock Stone was venerated as a sacred place. On the ancient Pagan festival of Beltane (1 May), a fire was lit on top of the stone in a bid to guide the good spirits back to earth.

bone-related problems and rheumatism, and several writers have suggested that the well was connected with rituals performed at the Hemlock Stone. This mysterious and charismatic stone has close connections with three other nearby stones: a standing stone on the nearby Crow Hill, the Cat Stone at Strelley and Bob's Rock at Sandiacre.

Another stone worth mentioning in Nottinghamshire is the Druid Stone at Blidworth, once thought to be a sacred place for druids, who gathered there to celebrate their numerous feasts. It is said to be an eroded glacial deposit, a mixture of pebbles, grit and sand fused together by limestone. It is over 14ft high and has a strange hole bored through its base. It is possible to enter it looking to the east. People once passed sick children through the hole in the belief that it would cure them of rickets, as well as numerous other disorders.

The ghost of a robed man (possibly Roman) has been seen at the site, standing beneath the stone. Strange purple and blue lights have been seen emanating from the outcrop, and one lady reports that the site is a favourite gathering place for fairies and goblins who meet, dance and hold high jubilee there.

Ouija Boards

The spirits of the dead, who stood
In life before thee, are again
In death around thee, and their will
Shall overshadow thee; be still.

Edgar Allan Poe

Ouija, pronounced 'wee-gee', is a flat surface printed or painted with letters, numbers and sometimes other mystical symbols. Placed upon the board is a glass pot or planchette (the planchette is the 'pointer' that is supposed to glide over the board, under the direction of supernatural forces, and form comments and questions by pointing to the letters), but any other movable object that can act as an indicator can be used. Other forms of Ouija board are used, especially the home-made versions, which comprise individual pieces of paper. The people present place their fingers on the glass or planchette and ask the spirits to come and communicate with them through the Ouija speculum. Some say that a certain number of people are needed and that odd numbers are better. If you are lucky, or unlucky according to certain schools of thought, the spirits will come and the indicator will begin to move across the board, spelling out messages from the dead. Furthermore, questions may be asked and answered.

Many believers state that the boards date back as far as 540BC. This is not entirely true, although there have been similar devices used throughout history and in different cultures. The true origins of the modern-day Ouija board are obscure. A man called

Charles Kennard and his Kennard Novelty Company first registered the Ouija patent on 10 February 1891. He called the new creation 'Ouija' because he claimed the board informed him that *ouija* was Egyptian for 'good luck'. This isn't true, but the name stuck and has remained to the present day.

Kennard began manufacturing the Ouija boards, which were also known as Egyptian luck boards, in 1890 – nearly a year before the patent was granted. He was so confident that the item would sell. It did sell in the thousands, and in fact the popularity of the board was incredible, partly due to the fact that the spiritualist movement started by the Fox sisters was gaining in popularity.

A year after this, Kennard was suffering financial problems, and William Fuld took over the company. He decided to reinvent its history and claimed that he had invented the board himself. He also said that Ouija was a mixture of the French and German words for 'yes', which is what most people today think the name means. All was well for a while until one fateful day when Fuld was overseeing a new flagpole being erected on the factory roof. He slipped and fell to his death. Rumours soon started to emerge that Fuld had thrown himself off the roof because he had been possessed by a demon that had been conjured via the board.

Ouija boards have also become an iconic part of culture, largely due to the fact that they appear a lot in horror films, magazines, books and contemporary folklore. The portrayal of the board has mainly been a negative one, and we are now intrinsically

Could such a simple arrangements of letters and numbers be responsible for inviting evil spirits into our homes?

programmed as a society to be immediately on our guard when we see or hear about them. However, there is resurgence in the use of the board. Teenagers are particularly drawn to it, fascinated by the suggestion that it is evil and dangerous. Some people seriously claim that the board is beneficial to them, giving prior knowledge of events yet to happen or warning them about dangers to loved ones. The board is also becoming a popular instrument of psychic demonstration at ghost walks and vigils; a practice which I personally frown upon as I believe it can be a very dangerous instrument, a bit like a power drill in a child's hands. Summoning spirits is the easy bit, it's getting rid of them which is often the problem.

In 1944 occultist Manly P. Hall, the founder of the Philosophical Research Society and an early authority on the occult in the 20th century, stated in *Horizon* magazine that 'during the last 20–25 years I have had considerable personal experience with persons who have complicated their lives through dabbling with the Ouija board. Out of every hundred such cases, at least 95 are worse off for the experience…I know of broken homes, estranged families, and even suicides that can be traced directly to this source…' Another major criticism came from the world-renowned mystic Edgar Cayce (18 March 1877–73 January 1945), who called them 'dangerous'. Critics firmly warn that 'evil demons' pretend to be cooperative spirits in order to trick players into becoming spiritually possessed.

There are thousands of stories circulating concerning bad experiences related to the use of Ouija boards, ranging from demonic possession, seeing apparitions of the dead, hearing voices and mental illness. Some go on to claim that Ouija boards are just as likely to cause psychosis as illegal class A drugs, which can cause drug-induced psychosis.

Christians believe that a Ouija board allows communication with demons, which – according to the Bible – is forbidden. Many people who have had evil entities take over their homes and lives have claimed that they only got rid of the malevolent spirit with the help of Christian Bible intervention. It is also widely believed by Christians that a dead person's soul cannot be summoned from the protection of God, and that what most people are actually in contact with when using a Ouija board are demons straight from hell. These demons, having been given access to the user, then set about destroying that person's life, and only Christian deliverance will save them.

In Nottinghamshire, I hear stories every week concerning ghosts and demons that have been summoned via the Ouija board, and many of those stories do not have a happy ending. The following is a selection of some of the stories, and as you will gather, it is not always wise to meddle with things we do not understand.

Story One

When I was in my early twenties a friend of mine introduced me to a friend of theirs who was very into the Ouija board. We went to her house, and she asked us to take part in an Ouija séance. I reluctantly agreed and she took us into another room, where she had a table laid out with candles and crystals. She didn't use a proper board, just some Scrabble letters and the handwritten words YES and NO, which were written in red ink on pieces of paper.

We attempted to communicate with the spirit world. Shortly after we had placed our fingers on the glass, it started to move. I was really impressed and the first spirit to make contact claimed to be an angel, who said I was a good soul who should not fear the burning plant, but should seek it out very soon as I would be in great need of it. Although it was weird, I was happy that a so-called angel had said that I was a good soul. My friend received a message from his dead sister which upset him. Later he teased me about the burning plant and joked about smoking marijuana.

A few nights later I was discussing it with friends and they all got excited and started saying we should do it again and make our own. My mum and dad were out for the evening and I had been left with my younger sister, but eventually, after much persuasion, I agreed. We set up our Ouija board and started. There were five of us. Just before the glass started moving, the room went very cold and we could see our breath, which appeared icy. This was really frightening as the central heating was on. Very soon, the board began spelling out messages for everyone – one got a message from her Polish grandmother, another got a message from his dad, and the others got messages from different members of their family. After they had left at 10.30pm there was a really cold atmosphere and there was definitely an eerie feeling in the house. Later that night I awoke in a heavy sweat and could have sworn I saw two red eyes looking at me from the corner of my bedroom, so I left the lights on for the rest of the night.

The friends that had been at my house told some of their friends about their Ouija board experience and word soon got around. The next time my parents went out (a week later), they all piled around to my house again and kept asking me to do it. In the end I gave in but with a sense of unease; somehow this time it felt different, definitely wrong, but we set up the Ouija board anyway.

As soon as we touched the glass it started moving around violently, and everyone kept accusing each other of pushing it. The board spelt out the name Shelley, and when we asked whether it wanted to speak to us it said yes but it wanted our blood. Startled, we laughed nervously and continued to ask it questions. It wouldn't answer whether it was male or female but said that it had been a murderer when alive and had committed suicide when the police were closing in on it. Then it started swearing and throwing abusive accusations at us all, but we laughed and tormented it – a huge mistake, as it just made it worse. It went berserk and raced around the table, eventually coming to an abrupt standstill. Then a most bizarre thing happened. The glass shattered into splinters – not just small pieces of glass, I mean splinters, and each and every one of us had a cut on our hand caused by the glass. But that wasn't the strange thing. As the glass shattered we could all see what appeared to be a bluish gas emerging from the glass and there was a strange smell in the air, like something burning. Everyone panicked and ran out of the house, and I was convinced something evil had just happened.

I didn't sleep that night and felt uneasy. During the night I could hear scratching noises coming from the loft, but I had no intention of going up there to find out what it was. Early in the morning my mum called me down and asked me why all the food was missing out of the cupboards and why all the tropical fish were dead in the living room (the living room was where we used the Ouija board). I said it wasn't me but admitted to having had friends around the night before, so blamed it on them. Dad was really angry and replaced his fish over the next few days; strangely, they just died again. He replaced them once more, but the next day they had all died!

Over the next few weeks things got really strange. We all kept waking up during the night. Fresh food would be found rotten the morning after it was purchased. Mum and dad started arguing a lot, and at one point dad nearly hit me; this was weird as he had never been like that with me in my life, and he got upset and cried. My little sister fell ill with some sort of chest infection that wouldn't respond to antibiotics; there were bad smells in our house; our pet cat of seven years went missing; the house became infested by wasps and mice; and my sister was having nightmares about a man with a knife – mum said it was because she had a fever, but I thought it was something else.

I just kept thinking it must be something to do with the Ouija board, so eventually I plucked up courage and told my mum. She didn't laugh and she wasn't angry, she just said 'leave it with me'. The next evening, I came home and there was a priest in the house. He said he wanted to pray with me, and after I had explained to him what had happened he asked me to help him, which I agreed to do. Next he sent my mum, dad and little sister out of the house.

He had with him a small bag, from which he took out some instruments. He handed me a silver-coloured stick with what appeared to be a pierced ball on the end. Removing the pin, he opened the ball, which was filled with some sort of moss or leaves, and he then lit it with a match and told me to follow him around the house. It was at this point that I remembered what the spirit claiming to be an angel had told me at the first session with the Ouija board, about not fearing the burning plant. The stick and ball thing I was carrying gave out a very strong-smelling smoke. The priest said prayers in Latin, and as we went into every room in the house he would sprinkle holy water and say more prayers.

After that day we were never bothered by that evil ghost again.

Paul – Watnall

Story Two

I used a Ouija board when I was 13 years old. I was with my sister, and we asked the board 'Is anyone with us?' The board answered 'Yes.' We then asked it to describe itself but it wouldn't and said 'You will see me next Thursday.' On questioning its response, it replied 'Go to the front door.' Spooked, we went to the front door and we could see an ambulance across the road at Genie's, one of mum's friends. We watched for a while, but being kids we got bored because nothing was happening, so we went back to the board and asked it more questions but nothing happened.

Later on, mum came home upset and said that she had been over to Genie's house to comfort her daughter and husband. Mum explained to us that Genie had died that day from a massive heart attack; she had collapsed in the kitchen. A few days after that, mum told us that the funeral was on the following Friday and we would all be going.

The following Thursday evening, my mum came up to our room and said we were to go out with her, and she took us across to see Genie's husband and daughter. When we got there, we were surprised to find about a dozen people there – we thought it was odd because they were drinking and laughing. Genie's husband came up to us and said to mum 'You can pay your last respects now', and mum took me and my sister by the hand, and we went into the front room. There, in a coffin with no lid on and candles around it was Genie. Genie was Irish and what we had visited was her wake (a celebration on the night before a funeral).

This event scarred me for life, and me and my sister still talk about how that Ouija board predicted what was going to happen. It must have been Genie's spirit that had been communicating with us.

Jayne – Radcliffe on Trent

Story Three

We lived not far from Nottingham Castle in a very haunted house. One day me and my cousin Jamie decided to play with a Ouija board that dad had found in the attic. We contacted a spirit who called himself Elijah Higgins. He said he wanted to play with us and said 'Don't be afraid of me.' He kept asking us about our family, then he started asking really personal private stuff, so we stopped playing on it.

My cousin stayed at our house that night, and we had a fun evening together. The following morning, when we woke up, we were covered in scratches all over our bodies. Mum put ointment on them and was really shocked. The strange thing was that they didn't hurt, even though some of them were quite deep. When she went to change the sheets on our beds, there was no sign of blood on any of the blankets or sheets, and we couldn't explain to her how we had got them because we didn't know. I definitely think we had come into contact with an evil spirit.

Louise – New Basford

Story Four

This happened to me and a friend when we were students. We were sharing a house together, and one night we decided to make our own Ouija board out of cardboard:

Me: Hello is there anybody there?
Board: Yes.
Me: Who is it?
Board: Help me I'm lost.
Me: What's your name?
Board: He won't let me tell you.
Me: Who won't let you tell me?
Board: The man that killed me.
Me: Please tell us your name.
Board: wedfgbhnjmicheloiujhgfcx
Me: Is your name Michelle?
Board: 1843.
Me: Is that when you were murdered?
Board: Yes, please help me.
Me: How were you killed?
Board: Blood, so much blood. Throat cut.
Flatmate: Ok this is creepy (she takes her finger off the glass).

I persuaded her to continue, which she did reluctantly, and we both placed our fingers back onto the glass:

Me: Hello are you still there?

Board: Yes.

Me: Why did he murder you?

Board: He won't let me go, I didn't do those things he said I did.

Me: What did he say you did?

Board: edfghjkl and lay with his friends.

Flatmate: Do you mean sleep with his mates?

Board: Yes. I'm cold please get my mother.

Me: Please tell us your name?

Board: Elizabeth.

Flatmate: What was the name of the man that killed you?

Board: I'm Robert.

Me: Are you the man that killed Elizabeth?

Board: Yes.

Me: Why did you do that?

Board: Now I'm going to kill you.

Me: Are you an evil spirit?

Board: No.

Me: Are you a good spirit?

Board: No.

Me: Then what are you?

Board: I am in the darkness watching you.

Flatmate: Why don't you switch a light on?

We started laughing at this point because what she said seemed so funny, but the spirit didn't like it.

Me: Are you still there?

Board: Sad and dead.

Me: You're sad because you're dead?

Board: No I'm sad you are not dead.

Flatmate: Was your family still living when you died?

Board: Yes.

Me: Do you miss them?

Board: Shut up I want you to die.

Me: Is there anything else you'd like to say?

Board: You have made him angry.

Me: Is that Elizabeth?

Board: Yes.

Me: Is there anything else you want to tell us?

Board: Danger.

Me: There's danger coming?

Board: Yes.

Me: When?

Board: Now.

Flatmate: In what way?

Board: Ask him about Jenny.

Me: Jenny who?

Board: Goodbye.

Just then my flatmate's mobile phone rang and we started laughing nervously. It was her sister, and she was telephoning to say that she had just seen my flatmate's fiancé in Nottingham city centre with a girl, and what was worse is that she had seen them kissing. Completely shocked, my flatmate spent the next two hours trying to phone him. Eventually he picked up the call and my flatmate told him what her sister had said and asked him where he had been. He said he had been out with friends and that her sister was a paranoid stirrer. At that point she just said 'OK, well if that's the case, who is Jenny?' He put the phone down!

About eight months later, we heard that her ex-fiancé had beaten his new girlfriend up (the same girl) and put her in hospital with a broken jaw bone. He went to court and got sentenced to a year in prison. Thanks to Elizabeth's message, my flatmate managed to avoid a potentially life-threatening situation.

Katherine – Nottingham city centre

The Whispering Dead

Wollaton Hall

Set in over 500 acres of historic deer park, Wollaton Hall is an impressive Tudor building, designed by Robert Smythson and finally completed in 1588, having taken over eight years to build. The hall is now home to the city's Natural History Museum. It is constructed of stone, supposedly exchanged for coal from the Willoughbys' coalmines. The family also made a significant amount of profit from the dissolution of Lenton Priory, as the stone was robbed from the priory and reused to build Wollaton Hall. The hamlet of Sutton Passey stood on the site prior to the hall but Sir Francis Willoughby, or should I say his greed, had the village destroyed to make way for his new project. In Elizabethan times, peasants had very few rights and even if their families had lived there for generations they would be forced to move on.

The hall was decadently decorated, both inside and outside, and no expense was spared. According to local legend, the outer walls have niches which were supposed to be occupied by elaborate carved statues; however, the ship carrying the consignment of fine carvings sank in the Bay of Biscay. When completed, the hall and park occupied some 790 acres, an avenue of lime trees lined the route to the hall and a lake was created. The whole park was said to be breathtakingly beautiful, and indeed it still is, with specimen trees planted strategically around the grounds. A deer park was added and a very adequate stable block, and in 1823

The Derby Road gatehouse at Wollaton Hall. Certain areas within the grounds are said to be home to the 'Little People', who have been sighted quite frequently over the years.

Wollaton Hall. Many ghosts haunt the building and grounds of this historic house. The mysterious room 19 is home to a ghost that is seen near to the window.

the hall's famous glass and iron Camellia House was added. In 1924 Nottingham City Council purchased Wollaton Hall for the sum of £200,000 from the 10th Lord Middleton.

There are many ghosts associated with the hall. The Minstrel's Gallery, in the main hall, is said to be regularly visited by a phantom that causes the temperature to drop rapidly. A previous worker was one day walking along the gallery when he felt the temperature drop – on reiterating his tale to other members of staff, they too came forward with other strange tales of icy blasts and doors closing of their own accord. Also reported was the sound of phantom footsteps, which could regularly be heard coming from one of the empty rooms in the upper portions of the building.

Room 19, as it is known, is believed to have been the former bedroom of Lady Middleton, who, after a serious fall on the stairs, broke her back and was confined to a chair for the rest of her life. After the accident she took to staying in her room, eventually dying in there, and since then her ghost has made regular appearances. On numerous occasions people walking in the park have reported seeing a myriad of twinkling candle lights coming from the room, and there can be seen the hazy figure of a women staring forlornly out of the window with a far-away look on her face.

The lake is haunted by two ghosts of people who drowned in the lake after deciding to end their own lives. No one knows why they killed themselves, but whatever gnawed at their souls to cause such a passing probably still does, as they remain here.

During the 1970s there were reports of small men being seen in the park; some people believe that they were aliens while others believe that they were the little people of supernatural legend. A 12-year-old girl described the little men as having long white beards and driving a bubble car, while others described them as being brownies. The spate of happenings continued over three months, and eventually they were seen no more.

St Giles Church, Holme

Nan Scott's Ghost

In 1665–66 the plague came to England, it quickly spread to other parts of the country and eventually reached the quiet unobtrusive village of Holme in 1666. This was the worst outbreak of plague in England since the Black Death of 1348. The earliest cases of disease occurred in the spring of 1665 in a parish outside the city walls called St Giles-in-the-Fields. The death rate began to rise during the hot summer months and peaked in September when over 7,000 Londoners died in one week.

There are three types of plague, but most of the sick in 1665–66 had bubonic plague. The symptoms were severe, with swellings (also known as buboes) in the lymph nodes located in the armpits, neck and groin. Plague sufferers experienced headaches, fever and severe vomiting. They stood a 30 per cent chance of dying within two weeks. This type of plague spread from an infected bite caused by a black rat flea that carried the Yersinia pestis bacteria. A much worse form of the plague was pneumonic plague, which attacked the lungs and spread to other people through droplet infection (sneezing and coughing). Septicaemic plague was also bad, occurring when the bacteria entered directly into the blood. These cases often proved fatal.

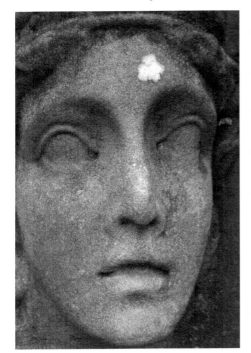

The miserable and emaciated figure of an old lady, Nan Scott, is still seen dashing around the vicinity of the church clutching a shawl to her chest.

There was no treatment for the disease at the time and all kinds of strange suggestions were thought up, including smoking strange and toxic herbs, pig's fat melted and drank in large quantities, fumigation of person and place with burnt feathers and holy waters as well as other unimaginable, as well as unpalatable, potions.

In Holme a woman named Nan Scott, convinced that the plague was sent by God to punish sinners, watched the village rapidly diminishing as day after day more and more funerals took place. Under the cover of darkness she packed up what few belongings she had and made her way to the church. She climbed the stairs to the tower and took up residence in a small room located in the roof.

Weeks passed and the villagers continued to die. Eventually there came a deathly silence over Holme. Nothing stirred, and not a

People once believed that plagues and pestilence were sent by God as a punishment on those that sinned.

single person was to be seen. Nan Scott, starving and weak, crept from her hiding place and went into the village seeking sustenance. The terrible silence and lack of people probably convinced her that the end of the world had come; terrified, she ran back to the church tower and locked herself away again.

The villagers were not in fact all dead; they had moved further into the countryside so as not to come into contact with infected people. In London, Charles II and his courtiers left in July for Hampton Court and then Oxford. Parliament was suspended and had to be held in October at Oxford, while the Council of Scotland declared that the border between Scotland and England would be closed. There were to be no fairs or trade with other countries. The fact of the matter was that the weather had also become colder, killing off the infected fleas and rats that accommodated the plague. Eventually the villagers made their way to the church to tell Nan that the crisis had passed, but unfortunately they were too late. She had perished in her holy fortress. Her emaciated body was removed from the church tower, and she was given a proper Christian burial.

After her death Nan's ghost returned to the tower, and during church services she could be heard walking about in the room she spent her last days in. She has also been seen scurrying around the village, as well as the churchyard. She is described as being very small, dressed in dark clothes and clutching a shawl to her chest. Her face is ashen white and her eyes stare out of her head as if she is terrified.

East Stoke

East Stoke, mentioned in the *Domesday Book*, is typical of many Nottinghamshire villages. It is quite unremarkable in a lovely way, yet it hides a secret — it was here that the last battle of the Wars of the Roses was fought. It is known as the Battle of Stoke Fields. On 16 June 1487 several thousand soldiers lost their lives in just a few hours. The army consisted mostly of 1,500 Swiss and German mercenaries, along with 4,000 Irish mercenaries. It was the beginning of a new age for England, and the civil war that had raged since the

1450s was at an end. The defeated army fled across the river and through a meadow known as Red Gutter, leaving their slaughtered and wounded comrades behind. Many were hunted down and killed.

Today the area is said to be haunted by the troops that lost their lives there. Conflicting stories have emerged concerning Roman soldiers being seen, as well as what are believed to be the dead of 1487. A lone soldier carrying a spear is frequently seen walking in the area, yet no one knows who he is. Strange lights have been observed dancing and swirling on Stoke Field and by the river, and on cold misty mornings the sounds of battle – swords clashing, horses galloping and shouts of anger – can be heard as if coming from a distant place.

A lone soldier carrying a spear is frequently seen walking the fields near East Stoke. Many battlefields have their own 'indwelling' spirits. These entities are said to be doomed by God to remain there for all eternity.

Ye Olde Bell, Barnby Moor

The Ye Olde Bell at Barnby Moor is one of the most distinctive hotels in Nottinghamshire. The building is set in a most attractive environment; it sits happily, if not smugly, in the heart of Nottingham's enchanting countryside close to Sherwood Forest. It has all the charm and character you would expect from one of England's oldest coaching inns, dark oak-panelled rooms, mullioned windows, open log fires and a warm, welcoming atmosphere. The surrounding area is steeped in history, and Nottingham and York are less than an hour away.

The Ye Olde Bell is believed to date back to the 16th century; however, some historians maintain that it was a much earlier date. In the days of the stagecoaches and highwaymen, the building rose to fame when local legend Dick Turpin stayed here, although this is heavily disputed. Stagecoaches started running between London and Edinburgh in 1635 when King Charles I inaugurated the postal service; it took six

The ghostly figure of a highwayham is said to be seen racing past the building, the phantom hoof sounds of a horse can be heard as if it is cantering very fast, it is accompanied by the cry 'Onwards!'. Travellers were once in fear of being accosted as they travelled to their destinations. Many were relieved of their valuables, some were murdered.

days to complete the journey. By the 19th century the Bell (then known as the Blue) was already a famous stop-off point for coaches passing between London and York. Remains of the old coaching stables may still be seen today, situated to the right of the main building.

In 1835 Queen Victoria stayed with her mother, the Duchess of Kent, at the inn. She was travelling along the Great North Road from London to a music festival at York. In the 1850s the hotel was used as a private dwelling, and many alterations were made to the building this time.

It is easy to imagine a ghost like Dick Turpin haunting the rooms of the building. There are actually many ghosts that haunt Ye Olde Bell, but perhaps the best known is that of the grey lady, who is intermittently seen in differing parts of the building. A previous worker at the building informed me that on numerous occasions he had experienced someone poking him in the shoulder. At times these phantom pokes were so powerful that they unbalanced his footing, nearly toppling him over. He also told me that chambermaids had often gone to attend rooms and, on knocking, they would hear a voice call out 'Come in', but on entering they would find the room empty.

The ghostly figure of a highwayman is said to be seen racing past the building. The phantom hoof sounds of a horse can be heard as if it is cantering very fast, accompanied by the cry 'Onwards!' but no horse or rider can be seen. As quickly as the sounds arrive, the phantom noises cease.

Bestwood Lodge

Bestwood Lodge is a Grade II listed building and was once the royal hunting estate of King Charles II and allegedly Nell Gwynn. This historical lodge is set in 700 acres of beautiful parkland, and only four miles north of Nottingham city centre. It is the perfect place to relax and unwind; many people love visiting the house for its scenery and friendly atmosphere, which gives it a unique ambience.

The original lodge would have undoubtedly been made of wood and plaster, and covered with slate and tiles. In 1683 King Charles II granted Bestwood Lodge to his illegitimate son Henry Beauclerk, the 1st Duke of St Albans. Henry's mother is believed to have been Nell Gwynn.

In 1363 King Edward III sent demands to Robert Maule of Linby, a custodian of Bestwood, to fell sufficient timber to enclose the park. He wanted to build a lodge on the most striking part of the enclosure – a place for the king to stay whenever he wished to hunt.

The 10th Duke, along with London architect S.S. Teulon, a leader in architectural design, built the house we see today. The original house was demolished in 1860 and a new and beautiful Gothic-style house, with red-brick and white-stone facing, was completed in 1863.

In 1893 a fire ravaged the building and the estate carpenter, George Fisher, discovered the drawing room ablaze. Knowing that the fire brigade would probably take some time to arrive, estate workers rallied around and set up a human chain to carry buckets of water to dampen down the flames. This was successful but a great deal of furniture, as well as numerous valuable paintings, was lost forever.

The ghosts are still very active and like to play tricks, often switching lights on and off again. Nell Gwynn is believed to haunt the building, and she is thought to make her presence known when families with children stay at the lodge. She manifests her presence through the scent of oranges, which can be smelt in several locations within the lodge.

A phantom Cavalier has been reported in the cellars, as well as a ghostly voice that periodically speaks to people. According to local legend there are bodies buried in the cellar, and it is their ghosts that can be heard whispering in the darkness. During the 1980s there was a spate of ghostly happenings, which were mainly manifested as random spirits seen wandering the halls, who would fade away when approached by members of staff. People wandering near to the lodge have reported hearing the lonely sound of a child crying. On investigation nothing seems untoward, and as they wander away the crying recommences.

Newark Castle

In ranks and squadrons and right form of war,
Which drizzled blood upon the Capitol;
The noise of battle hurtled in the air,
Horses did neigh, and dying men did groan,
And ghosts did shriek and squeal about the streets.

Julius Caesar, William Shakespeare

Newark Castle is located in the town centre, off Castle Gate. The castle is a magnificent 12th-century stone fortress, but sadly only half of this single-ward, quadrangle castle now remains. To the river front are the impressive remains of a range of buildings, while the north side is dominated by the oldest part of the building – a fine three-storey Romanesque gatehouse. The hexagonal corner tower stands to four storeys and contains an intriguing bottle dungeon, and in 1216 King John died in the tower.

The castle was built in 1133 by Alexander, Bishop of Lincoln, and it remained the seat of the Bishops of Lincoln until 1547, when Henry VIII confiscated it for the Crown. In the time of the Civil War the castle became an important Royalist garrison, holding out against three long sieges in 1643, 1644 and 1646. On 5 May 1646 King Charles I was captured at nearby Southwell and ordered Newark to surrender. The Parliamentarians then destroyed the castle, apparently with great gusto.

I was invited along to a ghost vigil at the castle. Usually I do not attend such vigils as I find them trifling and annoying, and there is only so much one can take when it comes to people shouting in the dark, 'An orb, an orb, I just photographed an orb' or 'Oh my God, did you just feel that? The room definitely just got colder'; but, fascinated by the history of the castle, I decided to go along. However, I did so on one condition – that people present were not informed about me and what I do. I find that people pester the life out of me with 1,001 questions when they know I am a psychic and write about the subject matter.

I arrived slightly early to get a feel for the castle; it was a charming place, which exuded a lovely feeling, and I felt quite comfortable there. One of the tour guides told us about the numerous ghosts that were said to haunt the castle. She went on to tell us about recent spectral activity within the building, but I had a sneaky suspicion that her story was slightly embroidered so as to make our ghost vigil more theatrically entertaining.

We took a quick tour of the building to locate where we would be returning to later. We had to leave King John's Tower in a hurry as one gentleman felt nauseous, which is apparently a common experience for people visiting that area. There were 17 of us in total,

Newark Castle, King John's Tower.

The ghost of King John is still said to walk this tower.

including six investigators and two spiritualist mediums. People were chatting, and there was a feeling of expectation in the air. After about an hour, and another two coffees, we were informed that the vigil had now officially begun and we were asked to follow our guide to the Undercroft. It was 11.30pm and we sat there in complete darkness. Suddenly someone claimed to have seen an orb (*big* surprise), then someone else said that something had just hit them, like a stone. Two other people then stated that they too had been hit by something; it was then that I felt something whizz past my ear and hit the wall behind me. Needless to say, I was not amused – if someone was throwing stones, be they dead or alive, they should not have been. Luckily it did not happen again. However, I did switch my torch on just in time to see one of the so-called mediums with their hand in the air as if about to throw something. I got shouted at by the other medium, who ranted about how people have supposedly endangered mediums by bringing their astral souls back to their earthly bodies too quickly when they happened to be in a trance. I tried to explain that I wanted to keep my eyes safe from phantom-thrown stones, and that no one was in a trance anyway, but they just looked at me in a patronising way. I really started to get the feeling that they did not like me.

Soon after this we split up into small groups, I ended up with Paul, an ex-Hell's Angel; Joan, a middle-aged housewife, and her husband Nigel, a bank clerk; and Janet, a nice Scottish lady who kept trying to feed me some of her home-made cake. We made our way through the gloomy night to King John's Tower. On arriving, everyone said that they could smell whiskey, and I just looked suspiciously sideways at Nigel who, strangely, was looking down at the floor.

Newark Castle. This charming castle is a magnificent 12th-century stone enclosure fortress. Very little of the original structure now remains, although its ancient ghosts persist.

Apparently the King's Tower was not only haunted by King John, but also by the spirit of a man named John, once a ranger at the castle. He kept antiquities there, and after the Town Council took the antiquities away he became clinically depressed and eventually killed himself by ingesting a lethal dose of rat poison.

While in the tower, Nigel said that he could see several orbs, while his wife Janet said that she felt the presence of King John standing behind her. She felt that he wanted to tell her he was not happy about dying at the castle and that he could not find rest. Also, we could hear a lovely chanting coming from the river side of the wall.

Next we went to the icy cold dungeons, where I admired the Knights Templar carvings. Everyone gathered and there was a session of table rapping: a process where a medium makes a table lift, or shift to the left or right – a bit like a Ouija board without the letters or numbers. Questions were asked, and answers came in the guise of table movements – to the left meant yes, and when it nudged to the right it meant no. The medium in charge slowly went through the alphabet, and when the letter M was said, it jolted. The medium asked if anyone present had the initial M, but no one came forward to claim it. The process was repeated again and it jolted at the initial L, but again no one spoke up. As it happens, I do have a nickname that begins with L, but I remained quiet. The medium continued 'Spirit what is your message?', and the table eventually stopped to spell out the words 'L please leave. You are amongst boglarks.' I couldn't control my laughter. The other medium, who was not conducting the table rapping (the same medium who had told me off earlier), became annoyed with me and asked me to stop laughing as it dispersed any positive energy that was currently present. I had to bite my tongue. I excused myself and left the castle immediately. You see, I knew who the message was from – he was Irish and always called me by my nickname Lussie. A boglark is the Irish slang phrase for idiot or gossiper, and he was referring to the others on the tour.

I left the castle convinced that it had ghosts. I could sense them everywhere; remnants of people that once were, shadows trapped within their tragedies. The castle is an amazing place, and I am sure that the spirits that dwell there will remain behind its crumbling battlements for some time to come.

The Palace Theatre, Mansfield

Originally this theatre began as a state-of-the-art electric theatre, and today it still has a reputation for excellence. It opened its doors to the public on Tuesday 13 December 1910 and was very well received. An all purpose-built cinema, it showed silent films and was an immediate hit. Prices for entry were charged at 3d lower pit, 4d pit, 6d pit stalls and 1s for the grand circle.

In 1949 the cinema was refurbished and the stage made bigger, allowing live performances to be shown there. In 1953 Mansfield District Council purchased the building, restored it and reopened it in 1956, calling it the Civic Hall. Further improvements were made to the theatre over a three-month period in 1963, and the façade and foyer were rebuilt, improving the aesthetics impressively. In 1968 it was renamed the Civic Theatre after Mansfield District Council offered a prize to the local community to come up with a new name.

The theatre is said to be haunted. Actors working on productions there often report the feeling of being watched. A pair of yellow boots were once observed to walk across the stage by themselves, and other strange phenomena include

Ghostly yellow Wellingtons have been seen to mysteriously move across the stage.

whispering heard coming from backstage when there is no one there. A man has also been seen wandering the back rooms; he is believed to be a former worker at the theatre who loved it so much that he still puts in an appearance every now and again.

Thrumpton Hall

Standing eight miles south-west of Nottingham, Thrumpton Hall is a brick building standing calmly next to the River Trent. It dates back to 1607, but incorporates parts of a much older building, built with a rose-coloured brick, which was occupied by the Putrels and built by the Pigot family, who lived there for many generations. There is very little information concerning its ghostly inhabitants; perhaps the spectres of this house like to remain private.

Viewed from the river, the building is relatively unimpressive, and one really has to go into the grounds to understand this house's unique quality and character. You will observe the gabled front with its unusual stone

The ghost of a Cavalier is seen descending the staircase. Many people have reported an oppressive force in the vicinity, as well as the feeling of being watched.

mouldings and the square and heavy-framed windows, which are a definite distinguishing mark of the architecture of James I's reign.

Thrumpton Hall is renowned for its superb cantilever Jacobean staircase, said to have been carved in wood from the estate. It is a massive and elaborately-carved staircase leading from the upper rooms of the house down to the basement, believed to date from 1660. It was installed by the Pigots, and their coat of arms may be seen on the staircase bearing three pickaxes, clearly a pun on the Pigot name, albeit vague. They were actually granted two coats of arms, and the other features a greyhound in a couchant position with a collar about its neck. The staircase is unique and perhaps the optimum example of its historical kind in the county. It was supervised by John Webb, a pupil of the famous Inigo Jones (15 July 1573–21 June 1652). He is regarded as the first significant English architect and the first to bring Renaissance architecture to England. He also made valuable contributions to stage design.

The ghost of a Cavalier is said to be seen descending the staircase. Also present on the staircase is an unseen force that makes one feel uncomfortable; apparently several people have felt as if they were being watched in the area. Beautiful phantom music has been heard coming from the library, which is believed to derive from a former resident of the house, Lady Lucy Byron, who was an accomplished musician.

Situated eight miles south-west of Nottingham, Thrumpton Hall stands calmly next to the River Trent. It dates back to 1607, but incorporates parts of a much older building.

The Phantoms of Park

The Park is one of the most remarkable residential estates in the United Kingdom and home to some magnificent Victorian architecture. It is perhaps one of the most atmospheric areas of Nottingham. The skyline is dominated by Nottingham Castle, and the estate once held the deer park and fishponds, as well as being a supplier of other precious commodities.

In AD500 the Saxons arrived and, ignoring the obvious Castle Rock, they decided to build their settlement where St Mary's Church now stands. In 1068 William the Conqueror espied the rock and ordered a fortress to be built on top of it, placing a man called Peveril in charge. Work commenced almost immediately. Nearby, woodland was enclosed to make a royal hunting ground which, together with the castle, was to be used by the kings and queens of England, their courts and visiting foreign nobility for the next 400 years.

The whole area is rife with ghosts; I have heard many stories concerning the spooky goings-on in apartments and houses. One house was besieged by a poltergeist that manifested itself by depositing rusty nails in the owners' bed every night at 8pm. A black dog 'with bristly uneven fur' was frequently seen on the landing, and growling noises were heard to come from the bathroom. However, on exploration of the room, it was found to be empty. Furniture was overturned and moved when the owners were asleep, and all the water taps were found turned on and running every morning, even when the main stopcock was switched off and the access to the drain it was housed in was heavily padlocked.

Other strange occurrences in the house included electrical equipment blowing up, voices heard coming through an antique clock and a strange white sticky excretion found

oozing from a wall. The house was exorcised twice before any relief from the strange phenomena was felt. On the second exorcism a growling was heard coming from the upstairs, and on exploration of the house the Latin words 'GRATE SALVERE' were scrawled on a wall in pencil which, according to the priest, roughly translate as 'Willingly I say goodbye.' It should be noted that these events took place over a short period of time, which lasted approximately just under three weeks!

Other ghosts include a phantom carriage and horses that is seen trundling about the streets; shortly after it manifests itself, a death is announced on the street of its sighting. A nanny pushing an old-fashioned Victorian-looking perambulator is seen on misty nights walking along the streets; you will see no baby in the perambulator though. The woman has a bloody hole in her cheek, which looks like a stab wound, and she is missing an eye.

The Besthorpe Miller

Besthorpe Miller is definitely one of the more beautiful areas of Nottinghamshire. It is a treat to drive along the lanes and roads taking in the beautiful countryside, yet hidden in this beauty are the ghosts of yesteryear.

Sand Lane was once the scene of a strange suicide. A windmill stood on the site in the 1840s. The owner was a man named Charlie – a hard-working miller who preferred his own company. Time went by, and Charlie produced ground flour for the local community, until one morning he was found stone-cold dead with a jagged cut to his throat. It was believed at the time that Charlie had committed suicide, although how he quite managed that remains unclear. No one knew if he had been depressed or upset, due to the fact that he kept people at bay.

Shortly after his death, reports began to surface that the ghost of Charlie could be seen wandering near to the windmill. Some claimed that the ghost appeared to be looking for something, while others maintained that his soul was doomed to wander the earth due to the fact that he had taken his own life. The windmill proved difficult to sell or lease, and eventually it was razed to the ground.

Charlie's ghost can still be seen today, wandering where the windmill once stood. One gentleman even stopped to ask him directions and, briefly looking away, he was amazed that the man had vanished; getting out of his car, the motorist checked the hedges and area to see if he could see the man he had spoken to but found nothing.

Annesley Hall

Hills of Annesley! bleak and barren,
Where my thoughtless childhood strayed,
how the northern tempests warring,
Howl above thy tufted shade.
Now no more the hours beguiling,
Former favourite haunts I see,
Now no more my Mary smiling,
Makes ye seem a heaven to me.

Byron

The majestic Annesley Hall, a Grade II listed building, is reputed to be one of the most haunted houses in England. It was here that Lord Byron bade farewell to Mary Ann Chaworth (1785–1832), some say the love of his life; however, this love was unrequited as she was already engaged to a man named John Musters. Mary Chaworth was the subject of at least five of Byron's early poems, including *Hills of Annesley*, and there are allusions to his

Annesley Hall. Reputed to be one of the most haunted houses in England, Annesley Hall is visited by a spectral old woman who ascends from a hidden well to walk the grounds.

love story in *The Dream* (1816). It was at Annesley that these two met as lovers. Byron had a bedroom there. The spot where that last sad interview took place can still be seen, and one can imagine the spirit of Byron continuing to haunt the seclusion of Annesley. Byron wrote: 'Had I married Miss Chaworth perhaps the whole tenor of my life would have been different,' and there was doubtless deep truth and meaning in his words.

Originally Annesley Hall was a hunting lodge; the hall was built in 1156 and has been added to over the years. It is set in a 17th-century landscaped park consisting of about 250 acres. William the Conqueror granted the Manor of Annesley to Ralph Fitz-Hubert, a Norman lord. The first Lord of Annesley Manor to take the name was Ralph Britto de Annesley, who died sometime between 1156 and 1161.

Numerous ghosts haunt the hall: an old man, a young girl, a haggard woman, a monk, an angry old man, a rather dapper man in a hat in the breakfast room of the house and a maid in a flop hat, as well as a young girl's restless spirit, who is thought to have fallen pregnant to one of the landed gentry and hanged herself at the top of the stairs in the laundry room. Indeed, many years ago, when the hall was being rewired with a new electricity supply, the remains of a pregnant woman were found underneath the staircase.

So-called psychic investigations at the hall have allegedly revealed firewood and stones being thrown violently about, while in 'Byron's bedroom' some people claim to have been pushed out of the room by unseen forces. Further claims of voices having been recorded in the monk holes have been made, as well as giant orbs and other light anomalies being seen all over the house. Whispers and snoring have also been heard in several rooms. The ghastly pale face of a woman has been seen at the window of the servant's quarters, and in the upstairs Lady's bedroom, visitors report a strange phantom flowery smell that comes and goes of its own accord.

Other spirits not at rest at the hall include a female spirit which is said to ascend from a well (now filled in). This spirit is seen wandering the grounds of Annesley as if looking for something. With its head bowed, it follows the track of an old bridle pathway, and other people have claimed to have seen the spirit sat in a tree, combing her hair in much the same way as fairies in Celtic mythology behave.

When I visited the area, I happened upon a lady walking her dog and asked her if she knew anything about the ghosts that are said to haunt the hall. She abruptly replied 'no', but added 'My grandfather does though – he worked at the hall for many years – he often talks about its ghosts,' and to my delight she invited me to meet him.

Jack was frail at 102 years old, but proud of the fact. He was remarkably healthy and lucid, and I remember thinking that I would like to be half as alive as him when I reach his age. He asked me if I wanted a cup of tea, Bovril, coffee or brandy. A few minutes later I was sipping my cup of Bovril and he began talking about his time in service at Annesley Hall. Eventually we came to the subject of ghosts:

She was always there, always watching, I think she liked me, because I remember cutting fire logs for the hall and looking up, and she was smiling at me, she just stood there cold-looking and unhappy, but smiling. We all knew that she came out of the well, several of us workers saw her crawling out, and dressed in rags she looked like a hungry spider; legs and arms crawling out of the well. To think about her is to shiver. I know if I went with you now she would be there watching me. She would stare at me like I should know what to do, should know how to help her, but I never did know what to do or how to help her. She saved my life a few times. Around 1948 I was hauling up some stone with a rope and pulley, and as I went to check on it she appeared and pointed at the ropes on the pulley, as I went to check them they collapsed, and the strange thing is I would have been stood under them at the time they snapped; like I said she liked me…Leave her be lad she'll be reet, she don't mean anyone no harm.

Enough said, I finished my drink and left, content in the thought that whatever haunts Annesley Hall is meant to be there and probably will be there for some time to come.

Calverton Village

Apparently the meaning of Calverton is 'calves enclosure', which suggests that Calverton was once better known for cattle-rearing than for being a mining village. Calverton is three miles north-east of Arnold. Considering the size of this village, I am surprised at the number of recorded ghosts it has. Clearly a great deal of history has taken place here, and the village cottages and houses have held on to some of their previous owners. The main street is said to have several ghosts, which are regularly seen out and about, including a red-haired man with very bushy hair wearing an expensive-looking tweed suit, a big black dog which has been described as resembling a Labrador, an old lady asking for change for a shilling at the bus stop – when you give her the money, she vanishes – and a pale-faced woman clutching a crying baby, seen scurrying from doorway to doorway.

In 1961 Calverton Hall, which functioned as a vicarage, was demolished to make way for the Miner's Welfare; some were happy about this as it had a reputation for being haunted, and many villagers would not venture near it after darkness. One villager informed me that it was common knowledge that when the hall was still standing, dogs would not go past it but would stand steadfast and bark angrily at it. Also, the ghost of a woman was often seen vanishing through a wall on the side of the building. One local, who used to be a bus driver, stopped one night near the hall to pick up a passenger, who duly got on to the bus and made her way upstairs. When the conductor went after her to collect her fare, he found the upper parts of the bus completely empty. The ghost may well be that of a woman who was murdered at the house some time ago. Apparently, in 1936 a skeleton with a hole in its cranium was excavated from one of the hall's rose gardens. Could this have been the victim of some heinous act? Did this skull belong to the woman that could find no rest? The ghost of the woman is still seen today wandering the area. She is known as the white lady, and according to local legend she was a maid that worked at the old hall. Having been jilted by her lover, she took her own life.

Another very haunted building is a stockingers cottage on Main Street, which dates from 1780. There would have been several thousand such houses and cottages scattered throughout the Midlands, as Nottinghamshire was home to a major cottage industry, supplying knitted wares of high quality to the rest of England and indeed the world. Silk stockings began to reach England in Tudor times. Henry VIII and later his son, Edward VI, were each given a pair of long Spanish silk stockings, which drew great admiration at court. Their successor, Elizabeth I, was presented with a pair of handmade black silk stockings in the third year of her reign; from then on she refused to wear cloth hose ever again. It was one of her subjects, a Nottinghamshire curate named William Lee, who in 1590 invented a hand loom known as the stocking frame. Within less than a century, knitting in silk was a well-established cottage industry located principally in Nottinghamshire.

Calverton Hall. In 1936 a skeleton with a hole in its cranium was excavated from one of the hall's rose gardens. The skull is believed to have belonged to the ghost of a woman who was seen walking through the wall of the old building.

The cottage is said to have two ghosts, as well as an aura of dread that is often felt in the building. At one time, workmen at the building refused to work there alone and would only conduct their work if they were accompanied by another person. Occasionally visitors to the building have heard the strange shunting sounds of a framework-knitting machine, and an old withered lady with a 'beaky' nose has been seen in the upper portions of the house. A malevolent force is said to sometimes occupy the building, and one can feel a discernible tension in the air, which is apparently quite frightening.

Another haunted building is the Admiral Rodney public house, situated on the main street between Manor Road and Old Hall Close. The inn was named after Admiral George Brydges Rodney, who was the victor over the French in the Battle of the Saints in 1782; this battle saved the West Indies for Britain. There are stories of numerous ghosts that haunt the building. The primary ghost appears to be that of a woman who haunts the cellars, turning off the beer pumps and rearranging furniture. The cellars are allegedly also the haunt of a little girl. According to local legend, there is a haunted tunnel that connects the inn to the old Calverton Hall.

Perhaps the village's most famous ghost is that of a black-robed figure seen floating about near George's Hill. One villager claims to have encountered the figure one foggy night as they were driving slowly down the lane. 'It was hovering in the air and as I approached the ghost it moved away out of sight behind a tree'. Also, people walking their dogs here feel a strange sensation of being watched.

In an area near to Oxton Road, which is where a gallows once stood (I have it on good authority that many criminals were executed here), the figure of a forlorn and unhappy man may be seen standing quite still and dressed in rags.

Sherwood Manor

The ghostly figure of a man in a hat and frock coat has been seen in several rooms of Sherwood Manor, a lovely old building located on Mansfield Road, Sherwood, Nottingham. This particular ghost is believed to be a former owner who lived in the building in Victorian times, which fits well with the style of clothing he has been seen wearing. Other ghostly happenings include furniture being moved around and things going missing, only to reappear at a later

The phantom figure of a man wearing a hat and frock coat has been seen in several rooms of the building.

date, nowhere near where they originally went missing from. Phantom footsteps are also heard, as if walking on floorboards, while a former worker at the building would frequently hear her name being called out when there was no one else on the premises. Another ghost said to haunt the upper parts of the building is an old lady whose appearance is always indicated prior to her arrival by the smell of lilac.

Residential Ghosts

Generally I try never to write about residential ghosts in my books. 'Residential' is a term I use to mean the ordinary dwelling places of the people of this shire; those houses that everyday people reside in. The reasons are numerous, but perhaps the most obvious is that very few people want to pick up a book and read that their house was once the scene of a gruesome murder or an unhappy suicide – some things are better left unsaid – trust me on that one.

There is also the fact that more and more people are asking whether a house is haunted or not – especially the older properties – and having a ghost can affect the saleability of a building. However, with so many people having ghostly experiences in their own homes, I rethought the situation and have decided to include some of those stories, as they appear to be of interest to my readers.

The following selection of ghost stories comes from the ordinary, often humble, people of Nottinghamshire who dwell in the estates, developments, flats, apartments, village cottages and leafy suburbs. Nevertheless, these stories are so interesting and intriguing that I feel it necessary to record a selection of some of them here for you. I have omitted very few details and have not in any way embroidered the reported facts of the ghosts or any other phenomena. The omission of certain details is to protect the individuals and hide the identity of the properties for reasons that I have already mentioned. I have transcribed the original details into a general format to make them clearer to read, but the information remains true to the original written interview with the person or persons concerned.

So sit back, pull up a chair, and let me take you on a tour of some of the homes of the Nottinghamshire people who have had supernatural experiences with creatures 'not of this world'.

Last Hour of the Dead

What I am about to tell you is completely true. I know it sounds silly and I do feel a bit uncomfortable talking about it. My grandmother was Polish, and she used to tell me and my brother ghost stories before we went to bed – not terrible ones, they were more like fairy tales really and usually had a happy ending. In one of the stories, she said that the true witching hour was 3am not midnight, as most people in this country believed.

My grandma died when I was 14; the same year this happened my mum inherited her house, which happened to be only 12 houses down from where we already lived. What happened took place just a week before we moved.

I was fascinated by ghosts, as was my brother, so we would read anything and everything we could find concerning them. When I was 14 and my brother was 12, we decided to stay up one night and go to the local cemetery at 3am. Gran had not long died and we thought we might even get to see her. My cousin Chloe, who was nine, had come to stay with us from Doncaster; it was school break time, so we stocked up on fizzy drinks, biscuits and chocolate and played quietly in my bedroom until 2.30am. We had flashlights, and creeping downstairs we made our way out the back door and went quietly down to the cemetery. When we arrived there we went through the wrought-iron gate, which made a loud creak like the ones in horror movies. We made our way to the back of the church, where the lights of the road just beyond the churchyard wall filtered through, making it eerie but not too scary.

We sat down in the midst of a huge yew tree that was more like a bush. I could see all the gravestones lined up, rows and rows of them, and not too far away was a big carved angel with a trumpet. We were comfortable and laughing in hushed tones when the church clock struck 3am. As the last chime died, we all held hands and I said 'We call the dead back from the grave, come to us in this your hour and speak with us'. My brother was laughing and making stupid ghost noises while waving his hands around. Just then, we heard the church gate creak really loudly and bang shut again. We sat there terrified.

After what seemed an eternity, we could hear the sound of footsteps on gravel and, peering out of the yew bushes, we could see a young boy about five or six years old. My brother called out to him, and he stopped then made his way over

to us. I asked him who he was and he said his name was Daniel, and he asked us what we were doing out so late in the cemetery. My cousin asked him the same thing back, but he didn't reply and instead asked 'Can I play with you?' It didn't seem that odd at the time; I mean, here we were in a cemetery at 3am, and there he was too.

We played for a while and chatted, and I remember Daniel telling us that his mum wasn't very well and his father didn't live with them anymore. He had golden wavy hair, a dimpled chin, lovely white teeth and cherubic looks. Daniel and my cousin were getting on really well, and she took off a cheap diamond ring she was wearing and put it on him, saying 'Hey, you can't keep it, but you can wear it for now.' He seemed delighted with it and thanked her.

We played I-spy, a game he didn't seem to understand at all, and my brother started talking to him about video games; again, he seemed to have no concept of what they were. About half an hour later, we started to get cold and tired, so I suggested we all go home. On arriving back home, I turned to Daniel and asked 'Hey, where do you live?'. He just pointed back in the direction of the cemetery. My brother invited him in for a bit, and we crept around the back of the house, went inside and made our way upstairs. When we got back into my bedroom there was no sign of Daniel, so I went back downstairs and looked for him. I even went out on to the street again, but I just figured that he had changed his mind and gone home.

The next day everything was back to normal, and we started packing boxes and getting ready to move down the street to my grandmother's house. Mum was in a panic trying to organise us, and my aunt was there helping with the packing. We were all having a break, drinking tea and eating biscuits, when there was a knock at the door. My aunt answered it, and on returning she said to Chloe 'It's for you, some kid called Daniel.' Chloe went to the door only to find nobody there. The rest of the day passed without incident.

A few months passed, and we saw our old house sold and the new people moved in. Then one night I woke up at 3am. I could hear the far off church bell striking the hour, and at the same time I was aware that someone was in my room. I squinted in the shallow light that was being cast from the landing lamp, and it was grandma! She was sat in the corner of the room on a chair. I wasn't scared, I was really tired and it seemed normal that grandma was there, it didn't even occur to me that she was dead and this was her ghost. I just said 'Hello Gran, are you ok?' then I turned over and tried to sleep. Moments later I felt her stroking my hair, just like she would always do, and then she said 'Send him back daughter, you must send him back,' I replied 'Send who back, Gran?,' but she didn't reply. I sat bolt upright in bed and suddenly realised what had happened – grandma had visited me.

The next day was a Saturday and when we were having breakfast there was a knock at the door, and mum went to answer it. I could hear mum talking to a woman and they were talking about our old house. I went into the hallway and could clearly hear what they were saying, they were talking about whether it was haunted, and mum was saying that she had never seen or heard anything in the house and it had been a happy house. The woman started crying and mum brought her in, they went into the front room and mum asked me to make coffee for them. When

I took the drinks in, mum said to me that the lady, Donna, would like to ask me some questions. I was terrified.

Donna was upset, because since they had moved into our old house they had been plagued by strange happenings. Apparently, every night since Donna and her family had moved into the house, strange things happened. They were all woken up at 3am on consecutive nights, by the sound of a man shouting, terrible crashing noises and a child crying, but on investigation nothing was found to be out of the ordinary. A coal bucket was also thrown against a wall, electrical equipment constantly went wrong and icy cold blasts of air would happen all over the house. There had been a strange buzzing noise coming from the attic, and on investigation it was found that six separate wasp nests were up there. One of them was apparently as big as a man. Pest controllers said they had never seen anything like it before, as wasps can be territorial and to find several separate nests in such a small space was rare. The family cat and dog had also gone missing, both on the same day, two weeks before. And Donna's two daughters had reported seeing a ghost; wherever they went in the house they would see it and now they were refusing to stay there. Donna had gone to a local priest, who was coming to do an exorcism on the house the following day, late on Sunday afternoon. Then she described the ghost and my blood went cold. She said that her daughters had described him as being young, maybe five or six, with golden hair and a dimple in his chin. As soon as she said 'dimple', I knew it was Daniel. Everything suddenly fell into place. We had definitely called a ghost back from the grave that night. Donna said that Daniel had spoken to one of her daughters and had asked where the other children that used to live there had gone. I denied everything because I was so frightened that mum would be angry with me and tell me off; worse still, she might ground me and not let me go on holiday with my friends the following week.

Later that afternoon I made my way to the churchyard. I wondered if I could locate a gravestone with Daniel's name on it. I was convinced that the ghost that was haunting our old house was his, and I kept thinking about what Gran had said to me, 'Send him back.' I searched among the headstones but couldn't find anything, but there was one bit I had left to check; it was very overgrown, full of brambles and ivy, just feet away from where we had hidden under the yew tree a few months before. The third grave I came to was partially covered with ivy and the stone had collapsed. I pulled back the ivy and there it was: 'Daniel Burgess – April 10th 1863 – June 11th 1890 – At Rest', and I knew it was him. I cleared some of the weeds away and made a clear pathway to the grave, as I intended to come back later.

I stayed up that night and waited; time seemed to really drag, I didn't dare go to sleep in case I overslept. I had this terrible feeling that if I didn't help Daniel then things would get worse. I felt responsible for what was happening, and I knew I had to do or say something before the priest arrived the next day. Eventually it got to 2.30am, and I started to make my way out of the house and go to the cemetery. I had my torch and had picked a white rose from our garden, which I planned to put on Daniel's grave. I waited in the dark, scared but at ease with what I was doing.

The church clock struck 3am, and on the last chime I placed the white rose on his headstone and said 'Daniel, I want you to come back and find peace, the people that love you are waiting for you, come back Daniel, find your way back.' Nothing happened and I just waited. Then the church gate creaked and slammed. I was terrified. I could hear the sound of light footsteps on the gravel path; standing there I didn't dare breathe. I waited for what seemed an eternity, expecting to see Daniel, but no one appeared. Eventually I moved away from the grave and had a very strong feeling that Daniel was going to be just fine. Turning my back on the grave, I had started to walk away when I distinctly heard a voice say 'Goodbye,' so I shone my torch in the direction of Daniel's headstone and something glinted at me. Going back to the headstone, I could see a diamond ring beside the white rose – the ring that Chloe had given Daniel to play with all that time ago. Daniel had gone back to wherever we had called him from, and from that day to this I have never dabbled in the occult again. I later heard that the ghostly things in our old house had stopped. No doubt the people credited this to the priest doing an exorcism, but I know differently.

Jayne – Edwalton

Author's Note: According to Judaic Christian belief, Christ was crucified at 3pm in the afternoon and it was widely accepted in the past, especially in other countries, that the hour of the Devil must therefore be the opposite, making the official hour of Satan 3am in the morning – the true witching hour. There was, and still is in some places, the belief that most deaths occur between 3am and 4am, when life is said to be at its lowest ebb. This hour is animistically known as 'The Last Hour of the Dead', when half the world is sleeping and half the world is waking up, yet some in the world are leaving and many are arriving.

Musical Ghosts

Many years ago we moved into a lovely old house in Netherfield, and an old lady had lived there before who was 101 years old when she died, although apparently she died in a nursing home. During her life she had been an actress and a singer. After a few months something odd began happening. My son (14 at the time) said that he kept hearing a woman laughing and singing in the loft area above his bedroom. I tried to convince him that it was just the old walls reverberating sounds from elsewhere in the house, or even from outside.

Time passed, and about six months later I came downstairs to find my son asleep on the settee wrapped in his duvet. I just thought he had fallen asleep while watching our bigger television downstairs. However, it did happen again. Later that day my husband came into the house after he had been working outside and took me to an outbuilding; he wanted to show me something he had found. Pulling back some old grey sheets, he revealed a beautiful, obviously antique, upright piano and started to play Chinese chopsticks on the keys. He wanted to bring it into the house, and I reluctantly agreed. My husband placed it in the hallway but something about the piano didn't seem right; I didn't feel altogether at ease with it and got a weird feeling when I looked at it.

A week later my eldest daughter came home from university. It was the first time that she had visited us in the new house. My son insisted that she stay in his room, which wasn't like him as he could be a little selfish at times and for him to offer up his bed was very unusual, but I just thought he was being generous.

The next morning I found my daughter asleep on the settee; surprised, I woke her and she complained that she hadn't been able to sleep the night before because of the sound of music and someone singing in the loft above the bedroom. Every time she was nodding off to sleep, the music and singing seemed to get louder and louder. My son came in and said 'Told you mum.'

Later on I spoke to my husband about it, and he said that he would go up into the loft and have a look later that day, but what with one thing and another he didn't have time. Later that evening my sister visited with her new boyfriend and we stayed up late chatting. She eventually left at 1.30am. My husband went up to bed and I started switching all the lights off. Our kitchen is quite a modern galley one and we had double-glazed sliding doors at the end of it opposite the entrance to it. The hob lights of the cooker were on and I made my way through the kitchen to switch them off. As I approached the oven, I caught sight of something in the reflection of the double-glazed doors – there, stood behind me, was a thin woman in a dark blue old-fashioned dress. She had some sort of long chain of beads around her neck, her hair was swept up in a large old-fashioned bun and she looked quite elegant, yet she was hard-faced. Shocked, I turned around and in that split second she was gone!

I left the lights on and made my way into the hallway just in time to see my daughter coming downstairs wrapped in her duvet. 'That bloody music and singing again mum, it won't stop.' I told her not to be silly and she just told me to go and listen for myself, so I did. Sure enough, I could faintly hear someone singing, it was muffled but clear enough to be heard. I called my husband, who could also hear it, then my son and daughter came into the room and we could all hear it plainly. I didn't tell them what I had just seen in the kitchen, I just told my husband he had to go up there and find out where that noise was coming from. He duly went and got the ladder.

We all stood at the bottom of the ladder waiting for him to come down. We could all hear the strange music again and finally he reappeared. Climbing back down, he had a large wooden box under his arm and said 'I think this is what's been causing the problem.' He opened the box and it began to play a tune I didn't recognise. Turning the box over, it had a handle for winding it up, and my son pointed out that it was impossible for the box to have been the cause of the music as it would have needed someone to wind it up every night. Besides, it was a woman's voice he and his sister had heard. My husband joked about it being a ghost and just then we all heard the piano in the hallway begin to play of its own accord. It was playing some obscure tune, but definitely a tune, and we all froze to the spot. My husband went down first and we all followed. The music stopped as we got onto the landing. I told my husband there and then to get the music box and the piano out of the house, and he immediately moved the piano, aided by my son, and the music box.

The next morning, the events of the night before were playing on my mind, and I asked my husband what we were going to do. He just nodded towards the kitchen window and our garden, and as I looked out I could see smoke coming from a fire which, by the look of it, had been well under way for some time. Looking back at my husband, he just winked at me and said 'Sorted.'

There were no more ghostly happenings after that night.

Annie – Redhill, Arnold

Two Sides of One

I have lived in this same house since I was born; I am now 83 years old. It's a lovely house and it has always had a happy atmosphere. I do not live alone in my house, I live with a ghost called Dorothy who, on occasion, visits me and keeps me company. My husband died when I was 42. We never had children but I am never lonely as I have 'Dotty' to talk to.

This house holds a dark secret; it was once the scene of a terrible tragedy. I am not a very well woman. I have recently been diagnosed with an illness which is probably going to take me, but I don't care and what's more I don't want to talk about that, I want to talk about happier things.

I first started seeing Dorothy in this house when I was seven years old. My mother had told me off for ripping my nice new yellow dress and dirtying my nice white socks. It wasn't my fault, cousin Henry had told me to climb the lilac tree to pick lilac with him, and I had managed to climb halfway and was reaching for a bunch of purple flowers when I slipped. Mother was furious, and I was sent directly to my room. When I got to my room I cried, not because I was told off, but because I knew we were having nice biscuits, sandwiches and cake for tea, and I was going to miss out on all the fun.

I was still crying on my bed when I heard a voice say 'Why are you crying?' I looked up and there near the window was a girl in a white dress. She looked just like me, the same hair, same height and even the same eyes, but hers were green (mine are blue). I told her about cousin Henry and she just laughed. Then I asked her if she was related to me. 'Sort of,' she said, and I was happy with that answer as I liked her, she seemed fun. I asked what her name was and she replied 'Dorothy, but you can call me Dotty.' We must have chatted and played for hours and then I could hear mum's voice calling me from the stairs, so I quickly put my shoes on and went downstairs. Mum asked who I was talking to and I said Dotty; she just looked at me strangely.

As time passed I would spend a lot of time with Dotty. When me and mum went out shopping or visiting people I would often see her and we would wave to each other. Sometimes if I looked out of my bedroom window, I could see her on the street, just under the gas light, and she would just smile and wave at me. Years passed and we would talk about boys and school and other things. I did start to notice that when I asked her about specific things like what school she went to and where she lived she wouldn't answer me; instead she would change the subject, and I suppose because I found her so interesting I didn't care to pursue the topic.

The war came and went and I didn't see much of her at that time. I met a young man called James and we started courting. Things went well and we got engaged. One evening I was sat with my mother in the parlour, and we were discussing my wedding plans. Mother was talking about my friends and who we should invite. She was writing notes on cards and without looking up she said 'Do you remember that invisible playmate you used to have as a child?' I reluctantly replied 'Yes mother', and carried on with what I was doing. Mother went on to say that children's minds are amazing things when it comes to the imagination. I told her that I hadn't imagined Dotty and that I still saw her, albeit intermittently, and besides she couldn't be all in my imagination because she was all grown up now like me; as I had grown into a young woman, Dotty had too. But what I couldn't understand was why we looked so alike. It was at this point that mother confessed a tragic secret: I was one of twins. The other twin had died shortly after birth – and her name was Dorothy!

Mother was such a practical God-fearing woman, not given to flights of fanciful imagination. She told me that on many occasions she had passed by my bedroom only to hear the voices of two children playing and laughing in the room. She had not ever dared come into the room, but she firmly believed that whoever it was I was playing with was my departed sister, who meant me no harm; indeed, it was mother's belief that she was sent back by God.

The next time I saw Dotty was at my wedding. She sat on the pew next to my mother and uncle, and when I walked back down the aisle she smiled at me and blew me a kiss. I have seen her many times since then, when I have been unwell or unhappy. We don't chat, talk or laugh like we used to do, but that doesn't matter; she smiles at me and I smile back at her and feel safe in the knowledge that she has always been there for me.

Annie – Toton

Author's Note: Annie passed away four months after relating this story to me.

Intervention

In my house there are three ghosts. The first is an old lady. I saw her in the bathroom and she was combing her long grey hair. The second can only be heard coming down the stairs. My workmate got the fright of her life one day when we came to my house for lunch; as she sat there in the dining room (I was in the kitchen), she heard someone walking down the stairs and, looking up, she saw a pair of woman's legs descend the open-plan staircase and fade away as they reached the bottom. She described the legs as 'perfect and wearing 1950s style shoes', which isn't so strange, as a previous occupant's daughter died while living at the property in the 1950s. She was murdered by her boyfriend and placed on a rail track, which divided her body, to try and conceal the fact that he had strangled her. My friend, who still doesn't know this, refuses to come anywhere near my house.

The third spirit is more unusual. It throws things at my windows – including stones and occasionally a dead bird – rings the doorbell and knocks or posts rubbish through the letterbox, usually in the form of dead leaves and twigs. One bright and warm summer evening, my mum and aunty came to visit me, and we were sat in the

front room of the house. My aunt, who doesn't believe in ghosts whatsoever, was sat in the bay window and from that particular armchair you can see my front door quite clearly. After half an hour my mum mentioned the presence in the house. My aunt threw her eyes up, tutted and said 'that reminds me, I've brought some *presents* for the kids' and told us she was just going to pop out to the car and get them. We heard her call out from the hallway and, rushing to her, we found her bent over a very large pile of leaves, twigs and dirt just under the letterbox – about a standard bucket full. 'Who would do such a thing?' she said and advised me to call the police, but I told her there was no point as it happened a lot, and besides she was sat right by the window and would have seen if anyone had come up to the door and posted it. We checked the door and it was locked, so no one could have come into the house and deposited the dirt.

The ghost of the old lady only tends to appear when changes are being made within the home. She was most active when I was adding an extension to the house. She would appear in the reflections of things – mirrors, doors and windows – my daughter even saw her through the reflection of our steel kettle. I know she doesn't mean us any harm, in fact I think she looks after us. When my son was 18 months old, I had not long put him to bed and had just sat down to have a cup of tea when I saw the old lady's reflection in the glass on the kitchen door. At the same time, there came a terrible crash from upstairs. I rushed upstairs, and there was nothing untoward until I went into my son's bedroom and found him not breathing. He was purple, and I immediately checked his mouth and found a small plastic toy stuck at the back of his throat, which I managed to remove. He luckily started breathing again and crying, but I phoned an ambulance anyway and within 15 minutes it had arrived. Meanwhile, my sister who lived nearby came over. The ambulance men arrived and checked him over, all was fine. There were two ambulance men and as they left, one of them turned around and said 'I didn't say goodbye to your Gran, she looked so terrified, is she alright?' My sister and I must have looked really confused, he went on to explain that when he arrived an elderly lady with long grey hair had let them into the house. She didn't say anything, she just pointed upstairs. I thought my sister had let them in, but she was in the kitchen and thought I had come downstairs to let them in. I am convinced that the ghost of the old lady saved my son's life that night. I still see her and every so often I make her a cup of tea, leave it on the side and say thank you to her.

Angela – Worksop

Author's Note: Paranormal activity is often reported to be more prevalent when changes, especially structural ones, are being made to properties. It might have something to do with the 'Electro Magnetic Energy Theory' (EMET). This theory states that walls, floors, doors and wood contain dormant energies which, when activated, usually by being physically moved or disturbed, cause psychic phenomena to be released or a replay to take place from a prior place in time where massive amounts of emotional energy – hate, love, desire, want, need and fear – were once experienced. Thereafter they are stored until the disturbance of the building's fabric reactivates it again.

Two Bells

Three nights before my father's aunt died, my dad was woken up in the middle of the night by a knocking on the window. My father is a very deep sleeper; he usually states that he could even sleep through an earthquake, and he claims the knocking wasn't the first time that such an occurrence has taken place in that house. Three nights before, a work colleague of his had a fatal heart attack and died, and the same thing had happened; knocking at the window roused him from sleep while my mum, who is a very light sleeper, didn't wake up at all.

I have also heard the knocking on two occasions: one was the night before my friend Gemma was rushed into hospital with an asthma attack, and the other was when my grandmother died. I was sat watching television when I distinctly heard three knocks on the window. My friend Dave was there at the time and it really frightened him. I went outside, but the back gate was locked from the inside so there was no way that anyone could have come in. There is also a sensor light out

there and that wasn't on. Two days later we got a phone call from Ireland to say that my grandmother had died suddenly.

On another occasion we were having a small party to celebrate my older brother's graduation from university. He had several friends there, as well as cousins and aunts and a couple of uncles. Suddenly there were three loud knocks on the door and my mum went to answer it. She quickly returned, stating that there was nobody there and it must just be kids playing around. Half an hour later the same thing happened again. Nothing was said but my dad looked uncomfortable. It got to 9.30pm and my brother and his friends said they were going into Nottingham for a night out. Just before they left the knocking happened again; this time I went, again there was no one there, I looked on the street and there was no sound of anyone being around. As soon as I closed the door the knocking came again. My heart jumped and I quickly reopened the door, but there was still nobody there.

Later that night my dad woke me up and said that my brother had been involved in an accident. We were all upset and went straight to the hospital. Apparently he had left home when a friend picked him and his two other friends up and they had headed straight into Nottingham. They were nearly in the city centre when a drunk driver ran into them. My brother broke his arm, the driver had head injuries and several broken ribs and the two friends in the back of the car had minor cuts and bruises. My dad believes that the knocking at the front door was a warning that something bad was going to happen that night, and it did. Afterwards the whole family discussed the ghostly knockings. We all wondered who or what it could be.

A few weeks later my mum brought it up in conversation with our next-door neighbour, Mrs Grindle. She was an elderly lady, and the only time we ever really saw her was on a Sunday morning when her daughter came to take her to church. Mum was hanging out some washing and caught sight of Mrs Grindle through her kitchen window. Mum gestured to her and she came out, and mum brought up the subject of the previous owner of the house. Apparently a deaf man called Joe once lived in our house, and after his wife died he became an invalid and would frequently knock three times on the adjoining wall if he needed Mrs Grindle's help. One day he kept knocking, but she couldn't go to see him as she had dropped a fork which had cut her leg and she was bandaging it. When she eventually went to see him, she found him lying on the floor – he had had a seizure and died.

Not long after that me and my family were all sitting having Sunday dinner, we were laughing and joking when all of a sudden there was a knocking at the front door. We all just froze and looked at each other. Dad went to investigate, but there was no one there. That evening we all went to my uncle's house for his birthday tea, and when we arrived back home there was a fire engine outside our house. There had been a fire in the kitchen caused by a faulty light fitting. Someone had spotted the smoke and called the fire brigade, who had arrived just in time to contain and put out the fire. The whole house stank of smoke though, and it was months before we got rid of the burnt smell.

Six months passed and everything was fine. The kitchen and house was redecorated and life was calm again, until the knocking came back. It was Sunday dinner again, and we were all sat at the dinner table when it started – three knocks – we all froze and guessed that something terrible was going to happen. Dad went to the door and came back laughing, saying 'it was one of my friends'. The next night it happened again, but it was just my uncle popping in to see us.

When I got home from work the following evening I noticed something different about our front door. It had two doorbells, one on each side. I went into the house and asked mum and dad about it. They explained that whoever came to the door in future would have a choice of bells to ring and hopefully wouldn't knock. We all laughed about it, and so far it has worked.

Julia – Rainworth

Dead Again

My wife and I were driving back from a golf presentation; the journey took us down some old country lanes near to where we lived at Rushcliffe. The evening was cold and the sky clear, it was half moon, and we chatted about how beautiful the

countryside looked at night. As we drove around a particularly sharp bend, we encountered a thick white fog. I braked hard, rapidly slowing down the car, then crept through the mist. It soon began to thin, and I figured that we must be in some sort of marshy place, as the rest of our journey had been fog free. I had my full beam on, and I started to speed up again as it was getting clearer. We turned another bend and as we did so I could see a young woman dressed in a creamy white dress. She had long dark hair, a thin pale face, and at that moment she looked directly into my eyes. But it was too late, and my wife screamed 'Oh my God!' as the car hit the girl's body.

Only that's not what happened. Instead of a thud or a bang when the body should have hit the car, there was nothing! I screeched the car to a halt and got out. The road was wide and the strange mist that had been there just moments before was gone. There was no sign of anyone having been hit on the road. I had a large and powerful halogen torch in the boot of the car, so I went and got it and me and my wife walked both sides of the road looking in the hedgerows. There was nothing untoward.

We continued our journey and got home somewhat shaken. My wife was convinced that we had encountered a ghost. She described the girl exactly the same as me, but she said that she could see more clearly the bottom half of the girl and where the bottom of her legs and feet should have been there was just an empty space. My wife also believes that she saw the girl pass through the car; she described the experience as an 'icy blast' fleeting through the car. I didn't know what to think. I even considered phoning the police, but I just kept thinking about how stupid I would sound.

The next morning was a Saturday, and I got up and went into the kitchen of our bungalow. I went to put the kettle on and it was unplugged, so I plugged it back in and continued. I decided to have some toast too, so I got some bread and put it in the toaster, only to realise that this too was unplugged. I plugged it back in. I took my tea and toast into the conservatory and switched on the radio to listen to the morning news. The radio was dead. I checked it and it, too, needed plugging in. Shortly after, I decided to have another cup of tea and went back into the kitchen to put the kettle on, but it was unplugged again. I thought my wife must have come in and unplugged it, so I plugged it back in, and a few minutes later I went back into the conservatory to find the radio switched off and unplugged again.

It didn't take long for my wife and I to figure out that something was wrong. My wife, on rising from her bed, had found our digital clock, television and bedside lamps unplugged, something I hadn't noticed when I got up. As we moved around the house, we discovered no electrical appliance plugged in. I thought about our deep freezer in the garage, but strangely this wasn't unplugged, and nor were any of the power tools or the car vacuum, which I usually leave charging. My wife came out and as we puzzled over the events of the past hour, we both saw something white move very quickly past the door which led back into the main house. Going back into the house, there was nothing out of place and the front door was locked from the inside, so no one had left the house through that door.

My wife brought up the subject of what had happened the night before. She said that she believed that the events were somehow connected; the spirit we had encountered on the road must have somehow come back to the house with us. The day passed without further events until the next morning, when exactly the same things occurred again; however, the day after that nothing happened and everything was plugged in as normal. That night we were both awakened by a loud banging noises and we both sat upright in bed. We listened and then there was a sudden scream, which sounded like it was from a distance. Next we heard the sound of a door slamming and footsteps, which sounded like they were running down a flight of wooden stairs, along with loud clunking noises and then the sound of a door slamming again. As we sat there in bed, not quite believing what we were hearing, we both observed a shadow move along the bottom of our bedroom door. Jumping out of bed I went to have a look, but there was nothing there.

The next morning my wife said that she was going to telephone a friend of hers who had another friend who was a medium. I didn't feel all that comfortable about the idea but thought maybe it was sensible considering what had been happening.

When I came home my wife informed me that our friend was coming to visit us with the medium the following Saturday morning. For the rest of the week electrical appliances continued to be unplugged, and the ghostly white shadow made several more appearances – the clearest was when I was sitting reading a newspaper, and out of the corner of my eye I cold see a white figure standing in the room watching me. Every time I shifted my eyes to look at it, I found that it was no longer there. Eventually I gave up reading the newspaper as seeing the white figure made me feel incredibly uncomfortable, and I was aware that whatever the thing was, it oozed a deep unhappy energy.

The following Saturday arrived and my wife's friend arrived at 10.30am with her medium friend. We told him about the events on the road the night we were driving back home, about the next morning and how everything had been unplugged and about the events that had taken place the night we had been woken up by strange noises. The medium then asked if he could take a look around the house by himself. We agreed and he went off alone.

About 25 minutes later, he returned and told us that the night we had been driving home, we had indeed encountered a spirit called Hannah. She had apparently been killed on that road late one night in the late 18th century by a carriage and four horses. She was 21 years old. He went on to say that she had escaped from a cottage nearby, where a cruel man named Jeremiah had been keeping her against her will. It appears that she made her escape one night when he had fallen asleep after a heavy drinking session, which ended in him violently beating her. Unable to withstand his cruelty any longer, she had started to creep out of the bedroom when he woke up and pursued her. She had run down the stairs and out into the night, slamming the door as she went, but he had continued to follow. Panicking, Hannah made her way to the road and was ploughed down by a coach and four horses, which killed her instantly. Jeremiah, fearing that the law would somehow pin the blame on him, committed suicide by setting himself and the house on fire.

The medium said that he had spoken to Hannah and explained that she could not stay in our house. She had agreed to leave and said that she was sorry for causing us any upset. She was terrified that Jeremiah would find her and was trying to gain our attention by unplugging the electrical items. She was also afraid that Jeremiah would try and set our house on fire. The spirit of Hannah had followed us home because we had somehow, in the moment of colliding with her spirit, formed a psychic link with her; a spiritual bridge had been formed between us all.

The medium reassured us that everything should now be fine and left with my wife's friend. When they left, I asked my wife how much money she had paid him for that pile of rubbish he had just told us. She seemed surprised at the question and, calling me an old cynic, she stated that she hadn't paid him a penny. He had made it quite plain that he wanted no financial gain from helping us. I thought that we would probably receive a bill, but one never arrived.

After that day, there were no more ghostly happenings. Life returned to being peaceful and quiet. Every so often I would think about those events and Hannah and wonder what it had all been about, so unbeknown to my wife I decided to do a bit of investigating. I went out of my way to the place of our ghostly encounter, managed to park the car on the roadside and set off to see what I could find. I wandered along looking for any clue as to where a house might have stood nearby. There was a small bridge just inside a field, and it seemed that there might have once been a pathway that led over the field and climbed a hillside. I followed the pathway, went up the hillside and eventually came to an area that had a small outcrop of trees. Moving around the outside of the trees, I came to a slightly overgrown clearing. Searching among it I soon found remnants of what must have once been a house. I pulled back debris and pieces of brick and soon began to find fist-sized pieces of burnt wood and bricks. I needed no more convincing, so I went back to my car and drove home.

Mr & Mrs Bramcote – Colwick

Playful Demons

At the age of 14 my father passed away, and I went to live with my aunt in her house near Mapperley. My mum had passed away when I was just a little girl and my aunt, being her sister, was the last living relative I had. My aunt was a loner and had five cats. I think they were all she wanted around her, as she seemed to really resent me being there.

The house was set in its own grounds and had a huge rambling garden with a pond and rose garden, which in turn backed onto open fields. My aunty used to go to bed early, often around 7pm. I would try and stay up later, but she would come down and insist I go to bed too, so I would go up to my bedroom and just read a book until I fell asleep. One such night, it was winter and very frosty, and as I lay there I could hear a rustling sound coming from outside. Getting out of bed, I went and had a look. My bedroom overlooked the garden, and I could faintly make out a dark shape that was walking near to the garden pond; it was dressed in what appeared to be a black hooded cloak. It kept walking in and out of some laurel bushes, pausing for a few moments and doing the same again. Then I realised there were two of the figures and they weren't walking in and out of the bushes, they were actually chasing each other. Eventually it became so dark that I could no longer see anything in the darkness, although I could still hear the intermittent rustle of leaves as if something was brushing against them. I went back to bed but slept with my bedside light on.

The next morning I approached the laurel bushes with anticipation and, pulling back the branches, I could see something in the middle of the bushes. Climbing into the bushes I found a small circular piece of cut wood and a strange collection of artefacts, including what looked like a large bird's skull, stones, small bones and pieces of contorted bark. I left it all where it was and went back into the house to speak to my aunt about what I had seen the evening before and what I had just found; she said it was probably the neighbourhood children playing in the garden as they often did, and seeing as they didn't really do any harm she didn't stop them. She had come across some of the dens they had built at the bottom of the garden near a heavily wooded area before.

A few months passed and I was in my bedroom reading a book when I heard the same noises again, so I switched my light off and went to the window. This time the garden was quite brightly lit, due to the half full moon. Going to the window I could see the same thing that I had witnessed a few months before, only this time I could see a lot more detail. The two figures were dressed the same. They were quite small, judging from the height of the bushes, and they were moving in a peculiar way, very fast. I couldn't see their faces, but their hands were almost skeletal and pale with really long fingers. As I watched them, they suddenly stopped and both of them turned and looked up at my window at the same time. Where their faces should have been there was just a black hole. I panicked, put the lamp on and closed the curtains. I could still hear the occasional rustling from outside, and eventually I must have fallen asleep.

The next morning I went outside and had another look in the bushes, but this time there was nothing there. A few nights after that I woke up in the early hours of the morning, and although my room was very dark I could sense that I wasn't in there alone. From the area where my wardrobe was I could hear someone breathing, I tried to switch the light on and, as I fumbled to do so, I felt a hand gently grab my arm. I screamed and just as the light came on I heard someone chuckle, but as my eyes adjusted to the light I could see that there was nobody in the room but me.

From that night on very peculiar things started happening in the house. Electrical equipment started switching itself on and off, objects would get moved, and my aunt would accuse me of moving her personal belongings so that she couldn't find them. Her glasses went missing, only to reappear hanging from my bedroom door handle. One day my aunt got really angry with me and told me to stop placing her parents' photographs face down on the piano. She also accused me of going into her bedroom, taking her clothes out of the wardrobe and throwing them on the floor, as well as taking a crucifix off the wall and putting it in the study desk. Other strange things were happening – sudden flashes of light came from different rooms – but when I went to investigate there was nothing there.

Sometimes as I lay awake at night I could hear the rustling coming from outside, and I knew that the people wearing the black cloaks were back in the garden. I would go and look, but no sooner had I looked out of the window, then they would stop and stand looking up at me. On one occasion I saw something protruding from the back of one of them; it looked like a long tail.

Winter turned to spring and then summer, and the strange things were still happening in the house. If anything they were getting slightly worse. Even my aunt began to comment on some of the events; she had gone to the bathroom,

and on returning she asked me if I had been laughing outside and knocking on the bathroom door when she was in there. I explained that I wouldn't do such a thing to which she just nodded, and she looked worried, as if something was bothering her.

Once a year the village had a summer fair at the local hall and adjoining field, which housed lots of fresh produce stalls as well as games and competitions. My aunt had agreed to help with a cake and biscuits stall, and several other village women were coming round on the Saturday to help bake and prepare some of the goods. I helped my aunty and her friends prepare, then my friend Clair called for me to go to the fair. Laden with some of the cakes, scones, biscuits and tarts, we made our way to the village hall. We went onto the field and had a look at some of the stalls being set up. We came across a large tent with a woman stood outside. The grubby sign outside said 'Gypsy Fortune Teller'. Fascinated, we went up to the tent. The woman looked us up and down and said we would have to come back later as her mother wasn't ready yet and could not read us at that time. We wandered back over to the village hall, and I started helping my aunt with the stall.

A couple of hours later Clair came and found me and insisted I go with her to the gypsy fortune teller; she wanted to know who she was going to marry and if it was going to be Rob (the guy she fancied). Reluctantly, I went. When we got there the same woman was outside and she said to me 'My mother will see you now.' I explained that it was Clair that wanted her fortune telling, but the woman didn't seem to understand and just gestured me to go in. As I stood there, the sheet that was covering the doorway was pulled back and an old lady with a blue shawl wrapped around her head appeared in the doorway. She motioned me to come closer, which I did, and as I stood in front of her she handed me a little bag and then she smiled and spat at me and vanished back inside the tent. I couldn't believe it: I looked down at my nice navy blue dress and it had spit on it! Her daughter said 'You will be fine now, put the bag inside your house.' Clair, seemingly oblivious to what had just happened, asked the woman if she could have her fortune told, to which she shook her head and said 'No, my mother is too tired.'

I went back to the village hall, washed the old lady's spittle from my dress and felt completely disgusted. I didn't tell my aunt about it, and the rest of the day passed without incident. As we were leaving, I saw the gypsy woman and her mother and they just smiled at me as we passed; they made me feel very uncomfortable.

Back at home I remembered what the old woman had said to me, and I placed the small bag that she had given to me in my bedside cabinet. What's strange is that from that day onward the strange happenings in the house stopped and I never heard anything unusual again. The dark robed figures that I had seen and heard in the garden on numerous occasions never came back again, so whatever the gypsy woman had done and whatever is contained in that bag that she gave me has kept them at bay.

Caroline – Mapperley village

Authors note: Spitting to ward off or counter evil spirits is a common practice among many cultures and is commonly used to avoid misfortune. The practice of spitting on someone or something is said to be a strong repellent against the 'evil eye', as the evil and malice caused by witches, evil spirits and demons is said to be rendered harmless by the contact of spit. Spit was once also considered to be a universal antidote against all forces of darkness. The old practice of spitting on your hand before shaking hands on a deal was a ritual to ensure that no evil would befall the deal about to be made.

Groovy Granny

I hadn't long moved into my new apartment when I had decided to have a house-warming party. However, most of the other apartment residents were elderly, so the following Saturday I decided to visit each of the flats to warn them that there might be a bit of noise when I had my party and to apologise in advance for any inconvenience this might cause them.

I started downstairs at flats one and two. The first was an elderly gentleman who was quite rude and kept going on about the rats in the rubbish bins in the recycling block, and he ended up slamming the door in my face. The second was a middle-aged lady who kept shouting because she was deaf, so I guessed there would be no problem there. The neighbour on the same floor as me was a 30-something fireman called Paul, who just said 'Yeah that's fine, go for it mate.' I thought at this stage that two out of three wasn't too bad.

I decided to leave the occupants on the upper floor until the afternoon. Meanwhile, I went shopping and, while perusing the special offers on beers with the following week in mind, a thin lady with enormous teeth approached me and introduced herself as Christine from apartment five. She was incredibly chatty; she talked about her invalid mother and how she was involved in amateur dramatics; about Dave, the mechanic, across the way in apartment 30 who had just split up and was getting a divorce; about Miss Bristow in apartment six and what a shame it was that such an awful thing should happen to such a nice lady; and how terrible it was that we were all going to have to have new parking permits, because some of the parents from the local school were using our restricted parking areas while they went to get their children. After five minutes I couldn't wait to get away. Eventually I explained to her about my house-warming party, which she didn't mind about at all. She explained she was out that night otherwise she would have loved to have come, and suggested we could meet for a drink and chat another time – imagine my glee!

On Monday morning I was running late. I heard the letterbox and discovered a stack of letters. Most of them were for the previous owners, which I put to one side, but another one was handwritten and addressed to Miss Bristow. I knew Miss Bristow lived in flat six on the top floor, so I put the letter to one side and decided that I would take it up to her when I got home from work. Unfortunately I didn't get home early: I went out for drinks with friends after work and didn't get back to my flat until 9.30pm, when I figured it was too late to take Miss Bristow's letter up. I decided I would do it the next morning as I was only working a half day.

At 10am I took Miss Bristow's letter up to her apartment and knocked on the door. The door opened, and the woman smiled and said 'Hello dear, can I help you?' I explained that I had just moved into flat number 4 and had received some of her mail by mistake. She thanked me and invited me in. I accepted because I wanted to talk to her about my house-warming party the forthcoming Saturday.

Miss Bristow's apartment was really nice, bright and cheerful. She was quite a tall lady and wore a bright crimson scarf around her neck, a jade green dress and unusually high-heeled shoes for a woman of her age; I estimated that she must have been in her late seventies or early eighties. There were photos in frames scattered around the room and I noticed that in earlier years she had obviously been a very beautiful woman. I explained about my house-warming party the following Saturday.

'Marvellous,' she said. 'That's exactly what we want around here, a bit of fire, a touch of drama to give the old fogies something to gossip about.' I promised to keep the noise to a minimum and assured her that it would probably all be over by midnight. She laughed. There was something fascinatingly bonkers about Miss Bristow, and I decided there and then that I really liked her.

The following Wednesday another letter arrived addressed to Miss Bristow, so before I went to work I took it up to her. She greeted me with the same cheerful smile and apologised for the letter being delivered to my apartment by mistake. On the spur of the moment, I invited her to come along to the party on Saturday and she agreed. I don't know why, but I was delighted. She asked if there would be lots of dancing and did a little dance, and we both laughed. I had the urge to hug her so I did and said that I would look forward to seeing her on Saturday night.

The following Saturday came and everything went really well. My family and friends really liked my new apartment and admired its layout and location. At about 11.30pm people began to leave, and I started saying goodbye to everyone. As the last guest got up to leave I picked up a red scarf from where they had been sitting and held it out to them, but they said it wasn't theirs so I placed it on the side of the chair and proceeded downstairs with them to ensure that the bottom door would be locked and secured when they left. I was just closing the door when Christine from apartment five appeared in the doorway. I let her in, and she immediately began chatting about all sorts of nonsense. I was tired and just listened in a bemused way, and she asked how the party went. I told her that the evening had gone remarkably well, and it was a shame that nobody from our apartment block had been able to make it, although secretly I think I was relieved. I started to talk about Miss Bristow and what a lovely lady she was, and Christine butted straight in and said:

'Yes she was a lovely person, always well dressed, if not a bit too much on the young side, she liked her music you know, I could hear it through the walls sometimes, the living room wall is very thin. Such a shame when she died, I mean I had been away for the weekend and it's a horrible thought to think she was dead in that apartment for three days and nobody knew it, the apartment won't stay empty for long, her nephew was putting it on the market in a few weeks time as soon as the legal matters had been sorted out, still the funeral was lovely and there were so many flowers...'

I couldn't hear what she was saying anymore. I had suddenly gone numb, I knew there and then that the old women I had spoken to in apartment six must have been a ghost. I said goodnight to Christine, went back inside my apartment, closed the door and went straight to the chair where I had put the red scarf 10 minutes before, but it was gone!

Hugh – Forest Fields

Lexicon Mystique

Glossary of Terms

Animal Ghosts

Many paranormal investigators agree that animal ghosts do exist and believe that the spirits of animals survive the process of death. Elliot O'Donnell says in his book *Animal Ghosts* (1913) 'The mere fact that there are manifestations of dead people proves some kind of life after death for human beings; and happily the same proof is available with regard for a future life for animals; indeed there are as many animal phantoms as human – perhaps more.' Another school of thought believes that animals share a collective soul and that five, maybe more, animals at a time share one soul.

Apparition

An apparition is believed to be a ghostly figure that appears in human shape, looking and appearing as if alive. The tradition of apparitions goes back to the earliest of times and documented accounts litter the pages of history from pre-Roman times to the present. All world cultures and societies maintain accounts of apparitions. Some apparitions appear only when a disaster is about to occur, while there are also those reported to guard sacred places. Apparitions may not always be seen, but may be heard or felt.

Audible

An audible is a ghost that is only ever heard and not seen. It is a fairly common type of ghost, which can often be heard shouting your name or whispering in your ear. Many ghost investigators have captured random voices on tape, and these types of occurrence coined the term 'audible'. The most ancient audible spirit, although to some people she will appear in person, is the Banshee.

Banshee

The banshee, or '*bean si*' as this spirit should be correctly pronounced, is undoubtedly Ireland's most famous ghost form. Said to follow long-standing Irish families, she is more likely to be seen by the third daughter and is commonly thought to follow a family whose surname begins 'O'. The banshee is believed to appear prior to the death of a family member, and the sound of crying and wailing is heard during the night hours. The sound has been described as like a cat wailing but much worse. The spirit is often described as female and either a horrible old hag or else a beautiful young woman dressed in a green dress. A third type is ageless with black holes in place of the eyes and nose, and all three main types have long hair. In Scotland a similar legendary spirit normally takes the form of a drummer boy or piper and likewise often foretells death or misfortune.

Barguest

The barguest is one name for the phantom black dog. In appearance the barguest is as large as a calf, with long sharp fangs and claws, fiery eyes and a shaggy black coat. This spirit could also appear in the shape of a bear, and the name barguest is thought to derive from the German for 'bear ghost'. The barguest seems to have been a name used relatively widely for a supernatural creature that can change its shape, hence a shapeshifter. In common with many supernatural creatures, the barguest could not cross running water, and as a black dog it was often seen as a death portent.

Birds

There are many instances recorded of birds returning as ghosts. Birds were once believed to be messengers of the dead, and when a bird tapped on a window it was thought to be a ghostly spirit looking for another to join it. Some birds are believed to carry the souls of the dead into the afterlife.

Boggart

The name boggart is mainly used in northern England and describes a particularly nasty type of ghost. Boggarts are thought to have the habit of crawling into bedrooms at night, pinching, slapping and biting their unfortunate victims. They are described as fearsome to behold with sharp yellowing teeth.

Bogie

Another rather unpleasant spirit, fond of haunting children, hence 'The bogie man will get you.' In British folklore, bogies are black in appearance with ugly grinning faces, and they are short and hairy with a foul smell. They were once thought to be the most powerful form of ghost, as they had served the Devil. They often seem capable of wailing like banshees.

Brownies

Brownie is a widespread name for a fairy or supernatural creature. They are small in appearance and wear brown-coloured clothing. Like many mischievous spirits, they are thought to be attached to houses or families and can be helpful in menial household tasks. If offended they become malignant and mischievous, creating poltergeist activity and generally making a nuisance of themselves. To get rid of brownies, you are supposed to leave them a new cloak and hood.

Cats

Next to dogs, cats are thought to be the most common form of animal ghost. The ghost cat may have its origin in ancient Egypt, where the cat was worshipped. Historically, the Devil was believed to take the form of a cat. Likewise the many ghostly and often black cats haunting many houses in England are sometimes thought of as vice elementals: spirits that have never inhabited any physical body and may have been generated by evil thoughts, or else attracted to a spot by some vicious crime or deed.

Changelings

It was once believed in Nottinghamshire that certain otherworldly creatures kidnapped newborn babies, particularly those of good appearance, and exchanged them with old, emaciated, decrepit and ugly fairy creatures who were known as changelings. The abducted children were not assumed dead, but as living in a timeless fairy place exiled from the mortal realm. Sometimes a lactating woman was also abducted to suckle these kidnapped mortals and fairy babies.

Church Grim

The church grim is the guardian of old churchyards. It takes the form of a black dog and is thought to protect the dead from the Devil, demons and other nefarious supernatural creatures. The dog was often seen on stormy nights and was regarded as a portent of death. It has been surmised that the church grim is a folk memory of a sacrifice, and it was believed in the past that the first burial in a churchyard would have to watch over the rest of the dead, so a dog might have been buried first in place of a human. Phantom black dogs are numerous in Britain, and almost every area has its own variant. Although not all of these are thought to be derived from a folk memory of a sacrifice, the practice was once widespread.

Clairaudient

Clairaudients have the ability to hear disembodied voices of the dead or other entities. Normally they will foretell events yet to happen. Many mediums claim to hear these voices of dead relatives and then pass on this information from what they call the 'spirit world'.

Clairsentient

Clairsentients have the ability to be able to feel things in a divinatory sense. Many mediums claim this ability is merely a refined basic human instinct.

Clairvoyant

Clairvoyants have the ability to see visions of events that are yet to happen, are happening or have happened. Many mediums combine this ability with one or another psychic faculty.

Crossroad Ghosts

Crossroads have long been associated with hauntings and although it is not exactly clear as to why, a number of theories have been put forward by way of explanation. Some consider it is as a result of a practice in older times for murderers, criminals and suicide victims to be buried at crossroads. This practice was said to confuse the spirits and prevent them returning and haunting the living. The cross formed by the roads represents a form of Christian protection. Witches were also believed to hold ceremonies and practise their black arts at crossroads.

Dogs

Ghostly dogs are reported from all across the British Isles and vary widely in size. For example, in Lancashire they have a black dog called Striker and in Wales there is Gwyllgi. Black dogs also frequent graveyards and desolate moorlands. Like the banshee, they may foretell death or misfortune within a family.

Doppelganger

The word doppelganger is derived from German and is usually the expression for a ghost who is either still living or is an exact double of someone. Those who have experienced seeing their double are believed to be heading for misfortune, but a sighting may rarely indicate good fortune. They are often experienced by friends or family of the person they are haunting, but in a place where the living counterpart was nowhere near.

Drude

A drude is an ancient English expression for a nightmare ghost – normally that of a mature witch, well versed in the arts of black magic. They are able to insert their ghost into the dreams and nightmares of their chosen victim.

Ectoplasm

Ectoplasm is a strange substance believed to be extruded from the sweat glands and body orifices of certain mediums while in a trance. The word 'ectoplasm' or 'teleplasm', as it is increasingly referred to, is derived from the Greek 'ektos' and 'plasma' – exterior substance. Described like pale or white silk strands or a jelly-like material, it is able to form human-like shapes. Some investigators have claimed to have examined ectoplasm over the years and stated it be biological in origin but its present biology is unknown to man.

Elementals

Elementals are thought to be spirits which have never existed in physical form, unlike 'normal' ghosts and spirits which have at one time lived in a physical form, either human or animal. Occultists declare them to be ancient spirits which pre-date mankind and fall into four categories, comprising earth, air, fire and water. Elementals are often associated with woodland, mountains or uninhabited valleys.

Exorcism

An exorcism is an act of religious ceremony used to expel a spirit, either from a human host or a building. The ceremony is normally performed by a specially-trained clergyman who will often say prayers and repeat loud exhortations. It also involves burning candles or incense and the sprinkling of holy water. This is a modern version of the old Christian rite of excommunication known as the ritual of Bell, Book and Candle. Modern mediums also claim to be able to perform a similar act, normally without the trappings of religion, by physically contacting the spirit and convincing it to move on to another plane of spiritual existence.

Extras

This widely-used term describes faces or sometimes whole images of people who appear mysteriously on photographs. Often the pictures show a white, wispy substance, out from which a face is normally starting to appear. In the early days of photography many so-called 'Spirit photographs' were produced, claiming to show the faces of the dead. Subsequently many, if not all, proved to be fraudulent. In recent years the white wispy form itself has appeared more and more, often without the attendant face. These are often described as vortex pictures, as a faint helix form is often to be discerned within the white cloud. Some researchers have declared them to be pictures of spirit energies.

Fairies

Fairies or faeries are said to be small often invisible creatures. They can provide great help or great hindrance to people. The colour green is sacred to them, and they inhabit trees, hills and valleys. Fairies are frequently associated with ancient burial mounds or stone circles, and are similar in many respects to elementals.

Fairy Curses

If the fairy folk are particularly displeased with a person, they would cast a curse on him or her. The curses took many forms: the cows ran dry of milk or the milk was soured; the afflicted person became ill with a mystery disease which only a fairy doctor could cure; the person became crippled with either a minor stroke, which only affected the face, or a major stroke, which hit one side of the body. However, for major transgressions against the fairies, such as cutting into their mounds or cutting a fairy thorn, the penalty was death. In the past, precautions were taken against the fairies. Salt and iron are two substances the fairies cannot withstand, so sprinkling the ground around your house with salt could protect you from them.

Fairy Fauna

There are many fairy trees along the roadsides and especially at the crossing of roads throughout England. Usually these are gnarled old hawthorn bushes. Also considered sacred to the fairies were the oak and the ash. In addition, many magic wands were made from the rowan. It is considered a profanity to destroy them or even to remove one of their branches. Many different types of otherworldly creatures are said to dwell in the trees and plants of the fields and woods.

Fireball or Lightball

The fireball or lightball is said to move in a slow and smooth manner and are frequently reported in haunted locations and near to stretches of water. They are believed by some to be the souls of the departed returning to Earth in order to guide the souls of the newly-departed to the next world.

Galley Beggar

The galley beggar is an old English ghost often reported in the north of England and mentioned as far back as 1584, in Reginald Scot's *The Discovery of Witchcraft*. This fearsome ghost is described as being almost without flesh and bearing its head under its arm and emitting a deathly scream. The name is derived from the word 'Gallery' meaning to terrify, and it is likely to be encountered on country roads and deserted lanes.

Ghoul

Ghoul derives from the common name for a ghost in Arabic. Nowadays it is commonly used throughout the world to define a nasty or vicious-looking ghost. The ghoul is believed to gain sustenance from eating the flesh of corpses – hence ghoul is often used to describe ghosts that haunt graveyards.

Goblins

Goblins are also known as hobgobs, gobelins, hob-thrush, blobins, bogles, bogies, brags, boggarts. The word is derived from the Greek 'kobalos' meaning rogue. The term goblin can apply either to the ugliest members of the fae or to certain sub-races. Those fae numbered among the goblin sub-races include the Scottish Trows, English Spriggans, Welsh Knockers, Cornish Knockers, German Kobolds and Wichtlein, the Irish Phooka and even Shakespeare's infamous Puck. They grow up to 30cm and are covered with a thick coat of black/grey hair. The goblin is usually found wearing very dark-coloured clothes and a tall cap similar to that of the gnome. They can also appear as animals.

Often portrayed as the villains and troublemakers of faerie, goblins are not truly completely evil. Though they seem to have no moral code of their own, they are happy to enforce that of their human hosts. The miserly and lazy are apt to feel their pinch or find their rooms and possessions in disarray; goblins are pranksters and are known for rearranging items in the house, tangling horses, banging pots and pans, removing the clothes from sleeping humans, knocking on doors and walls, and even digging up graves to scatter the bones around. Mine goblins make knocking noises by striking pickaxes and hammers against the stones. To placate a goblin, one must leave out a bowl of gruel in the fireplace. When the goblin has eaten, he will help with any household chores that have been left unfinished.

Graveyard Ghosts

According to folklore, the first person to be buried in a churchyard was believed to return as a ghost with special abilities to guard the site against the Devil. Because the task was so great, a black dog or more rarely a cat was buried before any human so it would become the guardian of the dead. Ghouls are also associated with graveyard hauntings.

Gremlin

Gremlins have only appeared in recent times, and the word is believed to have originated during World War Two when pilots often reported strange goblin-like creatures in the aircraft with them. Gremlins were immortalised by Steven Spielberg in his highly-entertaining film of the same name, and today hardly a piece of machinery can go wrong without somebody blaming 'a gremlin in the works'.

Grey/Blue/Brown/Green/Red/White Ladies

These ladies are believed to originate in Tudor times when the Dissolution of the Monasteries resulted in a great number of monks and nuns being made homeless. Nuns at that time were frequently habited in grey. Many other investigators subscribe to the theory that grey ladies are similar to white ladies, while others claim the colour is related to the surrounding substance, wood, plaster, or stone which may contribute to the ghosts' appearance.

Hallowe'en

Originating long before the advent of Christianity, the Feast of the Dead is perhaps a better name for Hallowe'en. It was a time of great celebration for our ancient ancestors, who would light great bonfires to try and summon and placate the dead. The Christian churches tried to mask the true meaning of the celebration by declaring it to be All Hallows Eve, the night before All Saints' day. Modern witches still celebrate the night of 31 October by the holding of feasts and the performance of rituals.

Haunted Chairs

There are many reported instances throughout England of ghosts being seen in an armchair which they had a particular fondness for, or may have died in. The ghost of Lord Combermere was reportedly photographed in his favourite chair while his body was being interred nearby. Many legends involve chairs that cause death or misfortune to the sitter and chairs that result in the pregnancy of the female sitter.

Haunting

Haunting is used to describe a ghost or series of paranormal events which takes place on more than one occasion within the same building or at the same place. We refer to such a place as being haunted. Objects, too, can be haunted and subsequent owners may experience incidents that are paranormal. Haunted items include furniture, jewellery and even the bones of the deceased.

Headless Ghosts

Headless ghosts are believed to be the spirits of people who have been beheaded. Evidence also suggests that these types of apparition may be connected to the ancient practice of beheading corpses. Many graves have revealed burials with the decapitated head placed between the knees – perhaps in the belief that the dead would not come back to haunt the living.

Headless Horsemen

By tradition, the headless horseman is the ghost of a rider who has been ambushed or decapitated when riding swiftly. Others believe them to be the figures of ancient Chieftains who, having lost their heads in battle, still wander the earth seeking their lost heads. Headless coachmen are also thought to be either the victim of highwaymen or perhaps were decapitated passing under archways or low obstacles.

Iron

Iron is thought to be a talisman against bad magic, witches and evil spirits. It was used by many cultures in the past. Saxon burials frequently contained iron talismans to protect the spirit of the deceased in his journey into the afterlife.

Lemures

Lemures is the Roman name for evil ghosts. The Romans believed that the spirits of the dead often returned to haunt relatives and friends. Ceremonies and rituals were frequently performed by many cultures to prevent such spirits returning.

Leprechauns

Leprechauns are the famed fairy creatures who own a crock of gold, which they usually bury beneath the end of a rainbow, or some equally ephemeral and difficult-to-find spot. They are shoemakers by trade and are usually found outdoors in rural areas. They are described as no more than two feet tall, and it is thought that if you can keep your gaze fixed on them long enough then they are compelled to lead you to their crock of gold, although they always manage to wrangle out of such compromising positions. Even if you do succeed in gaining the crock of gold, it usually turns to nothing more than dried up old leaves the following day.

Leprechauns are noted for their fondness for alcohol, which is usually made from heather, gorse or other unusual herbs or cereals. The making of the drink is a lost art to ordinary mortals. They also have a great capacity to consume large amounts of ale and other intoxicating beverages.

Ley Lines

Ley lines or fairy paths are reputed to run throughout the length and breadth of Nottinghamshire. These mysterious underground lines of power are associated with magical, paranormal or unusual happenings. In some rural areas, as late as the 1950s and 1960s, people would consult a local dowser or wise man/woman to locate where it was safe to build their houses. There is even an instance of a house being torn down, because one of its gable-ends was discovered to have been built over a fairy path. Strange noises were heard throughout the house, and the sound of thousands of marching feet was heard in the downstairs bedroom on the north side of the house, which was the side which covered the fairy path. When the house was relocated a few yards south of its original location, all the disturbances stopped.

Materialisation

Materialisation is an ability claimed by some mediums to produce a visible spirit. One of the first recorded incidents of materialisation happened in America during 1860, performed by the Fox sisters, founders of modern spiritualism.

Mermaid Pools

Mermaid pools are also known as pools of doom or death pools. These are secluded ponds and lakes which are said to be haunted by a certain type of mischief-making ghost. Many people report feelings of sadness and melancholy near them, and most of these pools link to legends of people who have drowned and are lost forever within their waters. The legend may extend back to ancient times when water deities were worshipped in many cultures, a practice that often involved human sacrifice – the body being thrown into the water.

Olfactory Smell

Some ghosts manifest themselves through the sense of smell. Certain people claim an ability to sense their loved ones through smells such as Grandma's perfume, Grandad's pipe tobacco or just a heavenly sweet smell of non-distinguishable origin, which alerts them to the fact that they have a spirit presence with them.

Ouija board

The Ouija board normally consists of 38 figured cards arranged in a circle. The letters of the alphabet and the numbers zero to nine are represented, together with two cards with the words 'yes' and 'no' upon them. The name Ouija derives from the French and German words for 'yes', thus the name is translated as the 'yes yes' board. It is alleged to act as a mediator between the worlds of the living and the dead. A glass or pointer is used to indicate the letters and words spelled out by the spirits. The board also carries with it a fearsome reputation for demonic possession of those using it, although in more enlightened modern times it is now believed to be a form of dowsing.

Phantom Coaches

The phantom coach is thought by many to be a messenger of death, similar in many respects to the banshee or phantom drummer boy. The coaches are always thought to be black, and the horses are usually headless, as may be the coachman. The driver or passengers are often skeletal or hideous with fixed maniacal grins. Passing at great speed, it is frequently silent, and, according to legend, anyone getting in its way will be carried off to their doom. This almost exactly tallies with the ancient Norse legend of the eternal hunt for their gods of the underworld.

Piskies

There are a number of creatures particular to Cornish folklore, although their cousins can be found elsewhere in Britain under a different name and guise. One of these strains is the piskie, also known as a pixie in other west country counties.

The piskie is a general name for a fairy race or tribe in Cornwall. In appearance they look like old men with wrinkled faces, and are small in stature with red hair. They dress in the colours of the earth, especially green, using natural materials such as moss, grass and lichen. Generally the piskies are seen as cheerful creatures with a prankish nature, and they are said to be helpful but also mischievous, helping the elderly and infirm while sometimes leading the more able-bodied traveller astray on the lonely moors.

Poltergeist

The word poltergeist derives from the German verb '*polter*', which describes a noise caused by banging, knocking or throwing things around. Harry Price, in his 1945 book *Poltergeist over England*, describes them thus 'A poltergeist is an alleged ghost, elemental, entity, agency with certain unpleasant characteristics, whereas our ordinary ghost is quiet, inoffensive, noiseless and rather benevolent.' In all lands and all ages the poltergeist is mischievous, destructive, noisy and erratic. A ghost is described as haunting, whereas a poltergeist infests.

Psychic

A psychic is one who deals with the soul and mind, being a mystic, clairvoyant, telepathic or having the ability to be able to see into the future. This should not be confused with 'spiritual', which is often used these days to describe mediums who do not need to be psychic to be spiritual, but who do need to be spiritual in order to be psychic.

Psychomancy

Psychomancy is the ancient practised art of foretelling future events by the appearance of ghosts or spirits and deciphering what their manifestation means to the living.

Salt

Salt is believed from ancient times to be like iron as a universal panacea against evil spirits and all manner of witchcraft and the Devil. Salt is often used in rituals to subdue a ghost by being placed in all the corners of the haunted building.

Séance

Séances are normally conducted by mediums who claim to be able to contact the deceased relatives or sometimes the spirit guides of the particular sitters. The process sometimes involves materialisation, disembodied voices or knocking and rapping sounds. Séance is French in origin and means a 'sitting'.

Spectre

Spectre was once used simply as another word for a ghost, but nowadays is more commonly used as a descriptor for a ghost that is found to be explainable by hoax or natural occurrences.

Tactile Ghosts

Tactile ghosts are ghosts that make contact through the sense of touching, tickling or pushing gently. Some spirits have been known to slap, punch, kick or even attempt to get physically amorous with people.

Talisman

Talisman is any object believed by the wearer or carrier to have the power to protect the owner from death or evil spirits. These charms are also ascribed the power to bring good fortune, wealth or good health.

Telepathic

Telepathic is an ability to read minds and know the thoughts of other people, either close by or frequently at great distances.

The Goath Shee (Fairy Wind)

The goath shee is believed to be a deathly cold blast of air that you feel if you cross over a fairy place, even in broad daylight on a warm summer's day. It can cause all sorts of malignities upon the unlucky person who feels it. Most often one is hit with a 'stroke', which can leave a person paralysed. It was also known as 'the blast,' and Shakespeare refers to it in *Macbeth* when he writes:

'And pity, like a naked newborn babe
Striding the blast, or heaven's cherubim horsed
Upon the sightless couriers of the air,
Shall blow the horrid deed in every eye,
That tears shall drown the wind…'
(Act I, sc. 7, 21–25)

Trance

A trance is an altered state of consciousness described as being somewhere between sleep and wakefulness. In this state mediums claim to be able to use their bodies or minds as a channel for waiting spirits or even healing energies.

The Stray Sod

If anyone chanced to walk over some enchanted fairy ground, they immediately lost their way sometimes becoming lost in a familiar field. This piece of land was known as the stray sod, as it led you astray. Also if any fairy beings had a mind they would lead you astray, and you had to follow wherever they led you against your own will.

Vengeful Spirits

There are many recorded instances of ghosts returning to avenge themselves of terrible wrongs that were done to them in life. These are known as vengeful spirits.

Wake

A wake is an ancient custom, thought to originate in Ireland, of sitting and watching over the dead while consuming large amounts of alcohol. This tradition is thought to help the spirit of the deceased in their journey into the spirit world. The practice of watching the body is done to prevent the dead body being entered by an evil spirit, and the noise of music, singing and dancing also helps to scare evil spirits away.

Warlock

The term warlock is used wrongly by many writers to describe a male witch. Many such witches would find the term insulting, as in the past the word also described a traitor.

White Ladies

White ladies are seen throughout the British Isles. Traditionally they haunt castles, mansions and old halls. A large percentage also frequent water and are seen on bridges or near to open stretches of still or slow-moving water.

Witch

A witch is a person, normally a woman, who practises witchcraft. There are many forms of witches, but most worship nature and call upon gods of fertility to help them with their undertakings. Witches are normally forbidden to tell anyone what they are, or how they practise their art, believing that silence is power, and power brings knowledge. Modern witches would not use their powers to harm people, instead choosing to help and promote spiritual awareness and greater wisdom of life.

Wizard

A wizard is a person, usually male, possessed with amazing abilities and well versed in the art of magic.

Wood Sprites

Wood sprites are the fairy elementals thought to live in the trees and the woods. They are the protectors of the wood and are particularly fond of the oak, the ash and the hawthorn tree. These trees were considered sacred trees to the ancient Celts and were not tampered with. Even in modern times it is considered unlucky to cut down one of these fairy trees, as the spirit who dwells within will wreak revenge on the offending party.

Wraith

According to ancient tradition, a wraith is the ghost of a person on the verge of death and often appear as an exact likeness of their human counterpart. They are regarded as a death omen, and should a person see a wraith of themselves, then their days are surely numbered.

Bibliography

Bord, J. & C. *Alien Animals* London: Panther Books, 1985.

Elder, Isobel Hill *Celt, Druid and Culdee* Covenant Publishing Co. Ltd, 1962.

Graham, J. McEwen *Haunted Churches of England*, 1989.

Hippisley-Cox, Anthony D. *Haunted Britain* Hutchinson & Co. Ltd, 1973.

Mathews, R. *Haunted Places of Nottinghamshire* Countryside Books, 2005.

Mitchell, W.R. *The Haunts of Robin Hood*, 1970.

Moakes, L. *Haunted Nottinghamshire.* J. Hall & Sons Limited, 1987.

———— *Haunted Nottinghamshire, Vol. 2* Happy Walking International Ltd, 1998.

Peters, J. *More Ghosts in and around Sutton* North Trent Publishing, 1995.

Pickford, Doug *Magic, Myths and Memories* Sigma Leisure, 1993.

Underwood, Peter *The Ghost Hunter's Guide* Blandford Press, 1986.

ND - #0304 - 270225 - C0 - 234/156/12 - PB - 9781780914237 - Gloss Lamination